Riding the Storm

Riding the Storm

My Journey to the Brink and Back

Duncan Bannatyne

BOOKS

Published by Random House Books 2013

2 4 6 8 10 9 7 5 3 1

Copyright © Duncan Bannatyne 2013

Duncan Bannatyne has asserted his right under the Copyright, Designs
and Patents Act, 1988, to be identified as the author of this work

First published in Great Britain in 2013 by Random House Books
Random House, 20 Vauxhall Bridge Road,
London SW1V 2SA

www.randomhouse.co.uk

Addresses for companies within The Random House Group Limited can be found at:
www.randomhouse.co.uk/offices.htm

The Random House Group Limited Reg. No. 954009

A CIP catalogue record for this book
is available from the British Library

ISBN 9781847941183 (hb)
ISBN 9781847941190 (tpb)

The Random House Group Limited supports the Forest Stewardship Council®
(FSC®), the leading international forest-certification organisation. Our books
carrying the FSC label are printed on FSC®-certified paper. FSC is the only
forest-certification scheme supported by the leading environmental organisations,
including Greenpeace. Our paper procurement policy can be found at:
www.randomhouse.co.uk/environment

Printed and bound in Great Britain by
CPI Group (UK) Ltd, Croydon, CR0 4YY

TO MY CHILDREN

Abigail, Hollie, Jennifer, Eve, Emily and Tom
Remember I love you more . . .

Acknowledgements

I would like to take this opportunity to thank those people who have helped me to survive the most tumultuous two years of my life. In particular I want to thank the directors of my company, Nigel Armstrong, Justin Musgrove, Steve Hancock and Chris Watson, who have continued to direct the Bannatyne Group. My fantastic PA Kim Crowther also deserves a special mention. I would like to thank my six wonderful children and, of course, my uber-cool son-in-law, whose help has been invaluable. I am very grateful to Lyndon Longhorne and his family, Ben Parkinson and his family, Noel and Liz Edmonds, Andy Reid and his family, Ron and Lesley Perry and children, Mark and Helen Burdon, Kim and Ian Wilson, Richard and Sandra Kimes, and Peter and Faye Jinks. My first wife Gail has always ensured my relationship with our children has stayed firm, and I am indebted to her for that.

I also want to thank my fellow dragons Peter Jones, Theo Paphitis, Deborah Meaden, Kelly Hoppen and Piers Linney, for putting up with my mood swings during that period. Finally I would like to thank Jo Monroe for working with me a seventh time; it has been an absolute pleasure. Thanks also to Harry Scoble and the team at Random House, and Jonny Geller, my agent at Curtis Brown, who has now sold seven of my titles.

Thank you to you all.

Contents

Introduction

When I was asked to write my autobiography in 2005, it seemed like the right time in my life to take stock and look back. *Dragons' Den* was starting to take off and a lot of people were asking me how I made my fortune. *Anyone Can Do It* explained how I had started out with an ice-cream van and gone on to build businesses worth £400 million. At the end of that book, I felt I was in a good place. A secure place. My businesses were growing steadily, I had enough money to do whatever I wanted, I had a beautiful villa in France where I spent quality time with my family and I was about to marry the woman I was deeply in love with.

I had no idea what was about to happen. We didn't know it then but the financial crisis was already rumbling towards us like an out-of-control freight train; and while I was thinking about the happy ever after, I think my wife was probably already considering divorce. Meteorologists talk about 'perfect storms' where a coincidence of climatic conditions produce devastating hurricanes. For me, the credit crunch and the divorce have created my own perfect storm. Though, of course, 'perfect' isn't the word I would use. Far from it.

ONE

In a Rich Man's World

The *Sunday Times* Rich List makes for very interesting reading, and like a lot of people, I can't wait to get my hands on it when it's published every April. For the past 25 years it has listed the thousand richest people living in the United Kingdom and if you compare this year's list with the first edition, it gives you a very useful snapshot of how the British economy has changed. It used to be dominated by barons and earls with all their inherited wealth, but each year the number of self-made entrepreneurs has steadily increased (as well as the number of footballers and pop stars, of course). To me, it's a really simple illustration of how Britain has become an entrepreneurial nation.

I sometimes wonder what I'd have thought of the Rich List if it had been around when I was a kid (of course, our family would never have bought the *Sunday Times* – we were a *Daily Record* household). I was born in Clydebank in 1949, the son of a factory worker. My dad always managed to earn enough to keep a roof over our heads and put food on the table but there was hardly ever anything left over. I can imagine him – a tough, hard-working WWII veteran – flicking through the Rich List and fuming at the ridiculousness of it all. His comments would all be about 'people like that': I don't think he would ever have believed his son would become one of *those* people. My wealth would have been beyond his imagination.

Every year, as you'd expect, the first thing I do when I get hold of the Rich List is look myself up (you would too, wouldn't you?). Have I gone up in the rankings? Down? Is the photo a good one? Then – as you'd also expect – I look up the other dragons. It used to be Theo first, then Peter. Now it's Peter first, followed by Deborah. Are they above me, or below me? Has their wealth gone up? Is it an unflattering photo?

The Rich List doesn't just tell us about rich individuals, it also illustrates a bigger picture, showing how the UK has become home to numerous overseas billionaires. Sometimes I realise that while I'm reading it I'm shaking my head in disbelief at how Britain has changed. You only have to walk round places in London like Kensington and Belgravia to see this: there are shops selling handbags worth more than the average house, let alone the average salary, and if you look in estate agents' windows you see gold-plated swimming pools and heated garages as part of the luxury spec. Indian steel magnates, Nigerian oil producers, Russian mining oligarchs: their wealth – Alisher Usmanov, who topped the 2013 list, is worth over £13 billion – is many hundred times my own, and their conspicuous spending highlights the massive disparity that has opened up between the poorest and the wealthiest in Britain in the past decade.

I enjoy looking at the list as much as anyone, but I'm aware that it encourages readers to judge people by how much money they have. If you look at any story about me in the press, it will always mention my wealth as if it's my money that's the most important thing about me. According to the Rich List compilers my wealth has fluctuated significantly over the past few years. In 2006 they put it at £168 million, but by 2008 it had almost doubled to £310 million. I think the highest valuation they ever gave me was £430 million, but then in 2011 it was suddenly £85 million. Had I become a less successful person overnight? My businesses had stayed pretty much the same size, I was still employing roughly the same number of people and still producing consistent revenues. Could I really have lost nearly 80% of my wealth? Surely I'd have noticed if I'd lost £345 million? I couldn't remember meeting Bernie Madoff, or putting all my money into Zimbabwe dollars. By 2013, I had dropped out of the list completely. Did that mean I was a less successful human being? Did it even mean I was a less successful entrepreneur? Of course not, and the reasons why wealth, value and cash do not always add up to the same figure is one of the reasons for writing this book.

The credit crunch, or the great recession, or the financial crisis – whatever you want to call it – has revealed that money is not the only way, and possibly not even the best way, to value a company. Lehman Brothers had billions of dollars on its books, Bernie Madoff owned hundreds of millions of dollars' worth of property, Woolworths had a turnover in excess of a £2 billion a year. In a period where almost everyone – including those on the first few pages of the Rich List – has been squeezed, it's the businesses with the small profit margins that have been the most vulnerable. Better to have a £500,000 turnover with a 50% profit margin than a £25 million turnover with a 1% margin.

It has been an interesting few years to be in business. Looking back, the first signs of the financial crisis came in the summer of 2007 when the word 'subprime' was featured in just about every news bulletin. American banks had started to realise that they had lent money to people who couldn't afford to repay it. Those people then defaulted on their mortgages, their homes were repossessed and the market became flooded with poor quality housing stock. Property prices crashed, bringing down the value of almost every house in America. Banks could no longer be sure that the assets they had lent against were worth more than the loans. To put it in layman's terms, they didn't know how much money they had.

At this point, I didn't sense any danger for the Bannatyne Group. I didn't see how the price of property in Detroit could affect my businesses. And even though the next milestone in the financial crisis was very close to home – those queues outside Northern Rock in September 2007 – I still felt insulated from whatever might happen.

My main feeling about the Northern Rock situation was actually relief, because there had been a time in the 1990s when I had deposited a cheque for £19 million into Northern Rock. If the credit crunch had happened at that point I might never have recovered; I wouldn't have had the money to build my health-club business; I would probably never have become a dragon. In fact, I'm only now beginning to realise just how lucky I was to start my business when I did, because when I speak to young entrepreneurs today it reminds me that you just can't do it the way I did it any more. But one of the great things about the events of recent years is that they have forced everyone in business to look for new opportunities and to be more creative. Although the past few years have been among the toughest of my career, they have also been some of the most exhilarating.

TWO

A Bit of Background

I suppose I should explain how I got to the point where I was depositing cheques for £19 million. I'll try and keep it brief – the full story is in *Anyone Can Do It* – but the danger when you tell a story quickly is that you make things seem easy. Believe me, earning that amount of money is bloody hard work.

There's nothing in my family background to suggest I would grow up to be an entrepreneur. As a kid, I didn't know anyone who owned their own business and most of the people in our neighbourhood worked at the Singer sewing machine factory round the corner. My dad had a job in the foundry there and he worked hard to provide for his family. I was the second of seven kids, and for most of my childhood my mum stayed at home to look after us.

I didn't just share a room with my brothers, I shared a bed. It was a way of keeping warm, as the only heating we had was coal fires. The Bannatynes never went without the necessaries, but we never had any luxuries either. I remember once asking my mum if I could have an ice cream and she told me no.

'Why not?' I asked.

'Because we have no money,' she said.

'Why haven't we any money?' I asked.

'Because we're poor.'

That was the answer to so many of my questions that my big ambition when I grew up was to be 'not poor'. I just wanted to have enough money to buy my family an ice cream. When I was told I couldn't have a bike, I decided I'd get a paper round and save up and buy one myself. But the lady who owned the newsagent's said she didn't need any help. I told her that my mum would like a paper delivered but no one delivered to our street.

'Well, I can't just create a paper round for one house, can I?'

'How many houses would you need?' I asked.

She scrutinised me. I could tell she thought I was a scruffy kid who probably couldn't be trusted. I could almost see her thinking of a number so big it would put me off. 'One hundred.'

I rushed back home, got a pencil and a piece of paper and wrote my mum's name at the top of it. Then I started knocking on every door in the neighbourhood until I had a hundred names on that piece of paper. I remember going home in triumph but all I got was a clip round the ear – I'd been out so long it had turned dark and my mum had been frantic with worry.

The next day, I went back to the newsagent's with my list

and I was given my paper round. It was my first taste of entrepreneurism, and a few months later I had enough to buy my (second-hand) bike. Of course, now I know that those hundred names were very valuable to a newsagent: these days I'd get the paper round *and* sell the list!

I was bright but not academic. I now know that I am mildly dyslexic, but as a kid I just knew I was struggling. Somehow, I passed the eleven-plus and went to the local high school, but this only highlighted how tough I found things. It didn't help that my parents couldn't afford a regular school uniform and I was sent off for my first day in a pair of home-made trousers and a borrowed blazer. That meant all the other kids knew I was poor, and I was teased about it or shunned. The only subjects I was good at were maths and woodwork, but even when I got the answers right in maths class I always got told off for not being able to show how I'd worked things out. I still calculate things differently from most people; my idiosyncratic method is fast and accurate – just inexplicable to anyone else!

Unsurprisingly, I was keen to leave school as soon as I was allowed to; at 15 I left Clydebank and my family and got a train to Suffolk, where I started training for the Royal Navy. At first I thoroughly enjoyed it: I loved being so active, I made some great friends and I found out early on that all the girls really do like a sailor. And once I had got my first commission, I also started seeing something of the world – in South Africa I was taken to a big-game reserve and saw elephants and lions, and in Yugoslavia I experienced life in a communist country, where I found that everyone was incredibly friendly and just wanted to buy us all drinks. For a young lad from Clydebank the Navy offered incredible opportunities.

I joined the boxing team – I had always been a big fan of Muhammad Ali – and as I started to fill out I actually became quite good (though not good enough to stop my nose getting broken). I competed in an interdivisional bout on the deck of an aircraft carrier and won on points. I was due to go on and compete for the Navy against the Army, but I was discharged before that could happen.

Looking back, I suppose getting discharged was inevitable. I have never liked having people tell me what to do and I've often had run-ins with hierarchies and petty bureaucracy. Let's be honest, I much prefer to give the orders than take them, and in this case I found that the orders were being issued by an officer who hadn't earned my respect. But I had signed up for 12 years' service. The only way I knew to get out of what had started to feel like a prison sentence was to get myself dishonourably discharged. One night, our ship was hosting a party and the officer I had taken a great dislike to said something insulting to me so he could impress the girl he had invited to the party. My mate Brian dared me to throw this officer overboard.

In those days I could never turn down a dare and when the officer left the party I was ready for him. I ran at him, lifted him up and managed to get him over the rail, but was held back before I could free his grip from the rail and send him into the icy water 20ft below.

I served nine months' detention in Colchester barracks before being given my dishonourable discharge. So, at the age of 19, I returned to my parents' house with no job, no reference and no idea what I would do next.

I signed on at the Labour Exchange and was given the option of training as an agricultural fitter and welder – basically a mechanic for industrial machinery. I also got a couple of bar jobs and within a few months I found myself with a qualification, as well as money in my pocket that paid for some driving lessons. Once I'd passed my test and done up my Hillman Minx, I was ready to work anywhere in the country. For the next few years I went wherever the work took me – Brighton, Leighton Buzzard, Leicester.

By the age of 23, I had drifted back to Glasgow where I made ends meet by driving taxis. I used my income to rent my first flat – the first time in my life I'd had a bedroom to myself – and to buy second-hand cars. But instead of selling them on, I got other drivers to use them, and without really realising it, I had started my first business. It was while I was running this taxi business that one of my drivers knocked on my door.

He explained that my parents had been trying to reach me and that he'd had a call over the radio. He looked shaken and was obviously nervous.

'You need to go home.'

'Why?'

'Your sister is dead.'

It took me a moment to absorb what he'd said. 'Which one?' was all I managed to say.

THREE

Starting Out

My elder sister Helen died a few days after leaving Scotland to start a new life in Canada with her husband. They had got off the plane full of hope and excitement, but within a week her husband was accompanying her ashes back to Clydebank. At the time the doctors couldn't give us any explanation as to why a fit and healthy 25-year-old should suddenly drop dead, but I've since read so much about deep-vein thrombosis that I think a blood clot caused by the flight was probably responsible.

I believe that becoming the oldest child in the family had a massive effect on me, not just in terms of the terrible grief I felt at losing my sister and watching my parents mourn her, but because Helen's death had a psychological impact on me that it would take me years to understand. I suddenly felt responsible for my parents and my younger siblings, and I immediately knew that I needed to take life more seriously.

There's been quite a lot of research done on birth order

and the way it affects how successful people become. A huge majority of American presidents have either been first-born or only children, and of the first 23 astronauts NASA sent into space, 21 were either eldest or only children. I am convinced that the tragedy of Helen's death is at least part of the reason that I went on to make a success of myself.

In the years immediately afterwards, grief made my behaviour erratic. I got into trouble with the police and drifted from job to job. But through it all I had a new determination to make something of myself.

Then I went to Jersey and thought I had arrived in paradise. It was a party island, and for five years I took any job I could get just to stay there – bartender, mechanic, ice-cream seller. It was only when I realised that I was in danger of becoming the oldest swinger in town that I decided it was time to make some changes in my life.

I remember sitting on the beach with my girlfriend Gail and reading the paper. There was an article about a man called Alan Sugar who had made a million running a computer business. As I read it I couldn't see that he had anything that I didn't have. If he could do it, I thought, then why couldn't I? I put down the paper and turned to Gail, 'Let's go back to the mainland, start a business and become millionaires,' I said.

I'm pretty sure she thought I was joking.

We moved – temporarily, we thought – to north-east England, where Gail's sister lived. Our plan was to work as hard as we could to get some money together as we wanted to get married and start a family. But this was the late 1970s and we were in one of the most deprived parts of the country.

There were no jobs, or if there were you had to be a member of a union to get them. It's easy to forget what Britain was like back then, but there were regular strikes, frequent power cuts and a real sense that people should know their place. It would have been easy to be bleak about my future. But then again, I had absolutely nothing to lose and in some ways that's actually quite a fortunate position to be in.

I think it also helped that I was an outsider: I had no real connection to the north-east, and that meant I didn't have anyone telling me what I should expect, or what I should settle for. So I kept knocking on doors until one day I got a job in an industrial bakery where they made thousands of loaves a day for companies like Hovis and the big supermarkets. I worked every shift they offered, and happily worked nights as it meant I got paid more. I think it was time and a half for a night shift, and if I did extra shifts over my regular hours, I'd actually get double time. It was great to be working like that because I knew I'd earn twice as much for my last hour as I had for my first.

The pay was tiered that way because it was a highly unionised factory, but when my colleagues went on strike to get even more generous terms I had no intention of joining them. They were doing things like calling in sick at the end of the week so their friend could have their shift and earn double time for it. The following Friday, their friend would call in sick and they would earn double time for covering them! I also knew that some drivers were taking vans out with extra bread in them and selling it privately. I can see now that this had an influence on me as an employer – we keep very close records of our stock levels. Even though I had been brought up in a Labour household, I didn't see any reason to join the strike because I thought we were being paid well enough already. They called me a scab, but I didn't care: I just kept putting money aside and little by little, the savings pot grew. It wasn't long before Gail and I had the deposit for a house.

I don't know why I wanted to buy my own home. My parents had always lived in council properties and I didn't know very many people who owned their own place (or maybe I did, it was just that home ownership and house prices hadn't yet become a national obsession). I remember having a conversation in the pub with a friend of Gail's sister.

'You're mad buying your own house,' I was told, 'taking on all that debt.'

'What you don't realise,' I replied, 'is that one day I'll have paid my mortgage off, but you'll still be paying rent. The way I see it you're in more debt than me.'

Ours was a very modest house that needed a lot of work, but I knew that by spending my spare time doing DIY I was adding value to it. I had also been making a bit of money buying up old cars at auction, fixing them up and selling them on for a profit. Sometimes when I look back at those days, I'm amazed about how much I was able to fit in – I wish I had that energy now. When young people ask me for advice, I tell them to make the most of whatever they've got: for me, that was the ability to work long hours and work hard. Not only did it mean I was earning decent money – I was already 'not poor' – but the cash I was able to get together in my late twenties was the foundation for all I would go on to earn in my thirties.

My entrepreneurial career finally started when I spotted an ice-cream van for sale at one of the many car auctions I went to. I stood staring at it for ages, thinking back to my days in Jersey selling ice creams on the beach. I remembered that on a good day you could take over a hundred pounds. I started to think about jacking it in at the bakery and setting up on my own. It was an exciting proposition, so I entered the bidding and picked the van up for £450.

I didn't know who I would buy supplies from, but I had a Yellow Pages so I phoned up local ice-cream distributors to find out who offered the best prices. I didn't exactly do market research, but it seemed pretty obvious that my customers would be children. So I parked near schools and drove the van to the kinds of housing estates where people bring up young families. I worked hard and pretty soon I started taking business away from my rivals. And when they threw in the towel, I bought their vans from them and employed people to sell for me.

I don't know why – and believe me, I've given it a lot of thought – I didn't stop at one van. After all, that's what most ice-cream sellers do. Why did I decide to operate a fleet of them? I can only answer that – to a simpleton like me – it made sense to do it. If you can make £500 a week selling ice cream and only have to pay someone £200 a week to do the selling, the real question is why doesn't every ice-cream vendor end up with a fleet of vans?

Pretty obviously, selling ice cream is a seasonal business, so I made sure I would have a year-round income by stocking things like milk and cigarettes. I also started to operate cafés in local parks where people bought burgers and cups of tea throughout the year. I worked seven days a week, and regularly didn't stop until 10pm, but by the early 1980s, I reckon I was earning about £60,000 a year. I had so much spare cash that I started to buy property. Britain seemed to be in a permanent recession at the time, and you could pick up terraced houses for around £10,000! It seems unbelievable now, but that's honestly how much they cost. I converted them into bedsits and rented the rooms out to DHSS tenants for £46 a week. I was making nearly a 50% return each year. I had five of them at one point. Again, I don't know why I became a landlord but the bigger mystery to me is why, with houses that cheap and guaranteed rents, more people weren't doing it.

In 1983 my daughter Abigail was born, and less than two years later Gail gave birth again, to Hollie. It was a fantastic time for me: I loved being a father and I loved that with the ice-cream business I had finally found something I was good at. For a kid who had done badly at school and who had never really felt he had any options, earning such good money and owning my own home was well beyond my childhood expectations.

By the mid-eighties, Britain was in the grip of what we now call Thatcherism. Among the people I knew there was a big divide: there were those who wanted to hold on to the past and stick with the trade unions that had secured employment for a couple of generations, and there were those who wanted to be their own boss.

The news was full of stories about the money being made by the barrow-boy bankers in their red braces in London, or the sell-off of council properties at reduced prices, or the privatisation of British Gas in which all of us were encouraged to become shareholders. Britain was changing and although I didn't really stop to think about it, I suppose I was too. It was around then that I first heard the word 'entrepreneur' and (once I'd looked it up in the dictionary) realised that I probably was one. And pretty soon after that I had another realisation: if I could run a small company, why couldn't I run a big one?

FOUR

Hard Work and Big Risks

A lot of people think that to succeed in business you need a good education, a good network of contacts, or financial backing. Even more people think that you can only really make a go of it if you have a brilliant idea or invention. I'm living proof that you don't need any of that.

For the first few years I was in business, my contact book was the Yellow Pages. I didn't have any special network and I found my business ideas where anyone else could have done – in the local paper and on the TV. Nor have any of the businesses I've started been unique – I'm not the only person who runs health clubs these days, and I wasn't the only guy selling ice creams in Stockton-on-Tees in the 1980s. What you need to succeed in business – and what I look for in the entrepreneurs who seek investment in *Dragons' Den* – is determination, self-belief and a willingness to take a few risks.

I do quite a bit of public speaking and at those events I

meet a lot of entrepreneurs. When I explain how I made my fortune, I often get people coming up to me afterwards saying that they could never do what I did. One of the great myths of business – and the myth I've tried hardest to demolish – is that you have to know everything about how businesses work before you start one. What those people who come to talk to me haven't realised is that I couldn't have started my health-club business without having earlier started the smaller ice-cream business. I wasn't born with the money, knowledge and contacts to start a big business – I gained all those things by running a small one. I've long said that you can only really learn about business by being in business. By the mid-1980s I had learned enough to start a much bigger and more ambitious business.

In 1984, the Thatcher government brought in a new piece of legislation called the Registered Homes Act, and when I watched a news report on TV about it, I instantly saw an opportunity. The new legislation would see the government pay a flat rate – almost exactly £140 a week – for every elderly person in need of residential care. I instantly calculated that a home with 50 residents would therefore have an income of £7,000 a week, making a turnover of £364,000 a year: in today's terms, that amount of money can't be far off a million. And unlike the seasonal ice-cream business, that income was guaranteed, week after week, year after year. It didn't matter to me that I didn't know anything about the nursing-home industry, because a few years earlier I hadn't known much about the ice-cream business. I knew I would learn. Millions of other people would have seen the same news bulletin as me, but I was the one who saw the chance to start a business.

I started by visiting care homes in the area on the pretence that I was looking for somewhere for my mother to stay. If I had been, I would have found the process profoundly depressing. I saw residents sharing rooms – sometimes as many as six women, who had all been strangers before they entered the care home, sharing not just a room but a commode. If I hadn't wanted to start a care home before those visits, seeing what went on made me determined to do so. I knew the care home I was going to open would give every resident their own room with en suite toilet facilities. I became a man on a mission.

I did the briefest of calculations of the costs involved – a classic back-of-the-fag-packet business plan. I estimated the utility bills I'd have to pay by multiplying what we paid at home. I found out what the statutory staffing requirements were – how many residents could be looked after by one carer – and then got a rough idea of salaries from looking in the Situations Vacant pages of the local paper. It wasn't any more scientific than that, but it allowed me to estimate that if my care home was 90% full, then I'd have a profit margin of 33%. That was over £100,000 a year. I became supremely motivated.

Gail was very supportive of my plans, and looking back I was incredibly lucky to have someone at home who encouraged my ambitions. She realised that if I carried on driving an ice-cream van every day, I would be working hardest when most people were spending time with their families – bank holidays, weekends and after school. As my girls got older, my desire to find something that fitted in with their needs grew stronger.

It quickly became clear that if I wanted to provide private rooms with en suite toilets, I was going to have to build a care home from scratch. All the existing buildings were converted houses with shared bathrooms and were often a warren of corridors and stairs – far from ideal for the people who lived in them. So I looked around for a piece of land to buy and found the ideal plot in an estate agent's window. Again, there was no special network I was plugged into – anyone else could have seen that land and bought it.

Finding the plot, which was in Darlington, was easy; getting the funding to buy it, however, was considerably harder. It cost £30,000 and although things were going well for me, I didn't have that kind of money just lying around. I was going to have to borrow it. These were the days when you still had a bank manager who knew you, and although I was regularly banking large amounts of cash and my account was always in the black, my bank manager wasn't impressed when I asked for a loan. He said the only way I could borrow was if I put down a deposit of £5,000 and offered my house as security. I was happy to do this. Gail, I have to say, was a bit more sceptical but backed me anyway.

I found a local architect who was thrilled to be working on something more substantial than an extension or a loft conversion. He saw working with me as a good opportunity, and I was happy for him to take on the responsibility for drawing up the plans and sending them out to tender – after all, I had no experience of employing builders or overseeing construction. Perhaps that's why I baulked at the architect's fee: 6% of the total bill.

'That's ridiculous,' I told him.

'That's standard,' he told me.

'But that means the more it goes over budget, the more it overruns, the more you get paid.'

'That's the way it works.'

'That's like paying someone for failure. I won't do it.'

So he and I arranged a fixed fee. That deal saved me thousands of pounds, and over the course of my career fixing professional fees – with lawyers, accountants, advisers – has saved me hundreds of thousands.

I seem to remember that the quote for building the care home was something like £210,000. So I went back to my bank manager and asked for a loan. When I explained that the business had a guaranteed turnover of £364,000 a year and realistic expectation of a third of that being profit, I expected him to calculate that I could easily make the repayments. He turned me down.

I went to another bank where I wasn't just turned down, I was insulted. 'If it was that easy, Mr Bannatyne, we'd all be doing it,' I was told. They assumed that I must have made an error in my calculations. I got the distinct impression that they thought I was a small-time ice-cream vendor with ideas above my station. I was now even more determined to make a success of it – and myself.

Eventually, the Yorkshire Bank offered me a loan, but there was a very big catch. They were prepared to lend me 70% of the value of the nursing home, but only once it was up and running and fully occupied. I was going to have to find the £210,000 myself.

The first decision I made was to scale back the construction. I had planned to build a 50-room care home because the regulations required that the ratio of staff to residents overnight was 1:25. If I had fewer than 50 residents, my staffing costs would be unnecessarily high, but that would have to be a problem for the future. My architect worked on a plan to reduce the size of the initial build to 30 rooms – we could add on the other 20 when I was able to get the loan.

My architect explained that the builders would be paid in instalments every six weeks when certain targets had been hit. When the first JCBs rolled onto the site, I really didn't know how I was going to make those instalments. I just knew that I had to find a way.

The ice-cream business was still doing very well, and I paid the first £20,000 out of profits. By the time the next payment was due, I had sold one of the bedsits, and I kept on selling them to make subsequent payments. Then I sold my car, my TV – anything I could think of. Somehow I managed to keep scraping together the money.

As the building took shape, I advertised for my first member of staff: a director of nursing. I found a manager who had worked for a rival, and when she learned that we were going to offer every resident an en suite toilet, she said she knew many residents who would want to move. She took care of all the statutory side of things and advertised for residents and staff.

It became clear that the ice-cream business was taking up 80% of my time but would soon provide a much smaller percentage of my income. It made sense to sell it, and two of my drivers bought it from me for £28,000. Not bad for a business I'd started for £450. It was actually worth a lot more than that, but as they could finalise things quickly, it meant I could make another payment to the builders.

Towards the end of the building process I was running out of options to raise the money I needed. I had disposed of every asset I had apart from the home where my wife and two small children lived. I managed to take out three credit cards and borrowed £10,000 on each. That bought me a bit more time, but it was still not going to get the nursing home built. I remember standing on site looking at the half-finished building and thinking that unless it got finished I was absolutely ruined. I went home and told Gail we were going to have to sell the house. I am eternally grateful that she said OK.

When I look back at the levels of stress my body was handling and the risks I was taking, I sometimes can't quite believe what I did. But I was just so sure of the numbers, and utterly convinced that opening a care home would be a great business. Some might say what I did was foolish, but experience has taught me that it's only when you're prepared to put everything you've got into a venture that you will have the drive and determination to make sure it succeeds. When entrepreneurs come into the Den looking for investment, one of the first questions they're asked is how much of their own money they've put into their venture: the more your financial future depends on the business, the more likely it will be that your business will succeed, because you'll *need* it to succeed.

When the end was in sight and there were just a couple of months left on the construction, I completely ran out of cash. I had absolutely nothing left to sell and no way of borrowing any more money. My worst nightmare was coming true. I had no option but to level with my builder.

'I've got a bit of a cash-flow problem. Can we talk about deferring the final payment until after completion?'

To my immense relief he didn't tell his crew to down tools. 'I knew you were having problems,' he told me. 'It's clear you've sold everything you've got. Here's what I'll do. I'll defer the payment until after you've got your loan sorted, but I want an extra 10%.'

I was in no position to argue. What I didn't realise until I checked the paperwork was that he meant an extra 10% a month! In retrospect, he could have been a lot harder on me and to his credit he carried on with the build.

Almost before the carpenters and electricians were off site, we raced to get the home ready for its new residents. I was in desperate need of cash and I wanted to open the home as soon as possible so that I could go back to the Yorkshire Bank and get that loan they had promised.

Although we opened pretty much on time and hardly over budget, we were not full. Knowing that I wouldn't get my loan unless I had 100% occupancy, I called up my mum in Clydebank. How did she fancy a trip to see her granddaughters? And would she mind bringing some friends with her? I'm not kidding: when the valuers came round I wanted to be absolutely sure that they would see an old person in every room. I think my mum and her friends quite enjoyed their day trip.

When I got confirmation that the loan had been approved my relief was immense. The business was valued at £600,000 and I was given a loan for £420,000 (the 70% I'd been promised). In total I had spent £360,000 on getting the home ready – that figure included everything from bed linen to credit-card interest payments. I cleared my debts and used the excess to build another 20 rooms. When I had 50 residents, I got the business revalued, increased the loan and immediately used that money to build another home. It was slightly more straightforward the second time, but not much.

Throughout the rest of the 1980s Quality Care Homes expanded rapidly and by the end of 1991 I had opened our ninth home. Our turnover was just over £3 million and we had debts of around £6 million. I wanted to keep on expanding, but it got to the point where the banks refused to lend to me. They wanted me to slow down, but I just didn't see the point. So I made the decision to float the company on the London Stock Exchange to get the money I wanted in order to expand. The business was valued at around £20 million, and as only 27% of the company would be offered to shareholders, that meant my stake was worth a little under £15 million.

FIVE

Realising the Value

After the flotation, I received a personal cheque for £500,000, which represented the number of shares I was allowed to sell. The investors and directors wanted as much of my wealth as possible to be tied up in the business. That was absolutely fine with me, but for a former council-house kid, a cheque for half a million pounds required celebrating, so I took Gail and the girls away for a ski trip. It turned out to be a very significant break – quite literally.

I took a pretty spectacular fall and snapped several ligaments around my knee. It required surgery to reattach them, followed by months of physiotherapy. The most important exercises I needed to do involved the use of a leg press. When I found out that the nearest gym with a leg press was half an hour's drive away, I concluded that there was a market for someone to open a health club closer to home. I didn't do anything about it for a couple of years, but the thought never left me.

In the meantime, I used the cash injection from the flotation to expand Quality Care Homes. By the mid 1990s, we were operating about 15 homes. Every six months I put on a suit and went to London to talk to investors. Everyone seemed very happy with our progress.

Things were also expanding on the home front: my daughter Jennifer was born in 1992, and Eve came along a couple of years later. It should have been a wonderful time for me. I adored my business almost as much as I adored my family and I had more money than I had ever dreamed of, but I found myself becoming increasingly depressed. My lowest point came when I was driving to an appointment and realised I had to pull over. I parked in a lay-by and started sobbing. I didn't know what was wrong with me or why I was feeling like this. After many months of soul-searching I finally acknowledged what was making me miserable – it was my marriage.

I don't know why, but I had fallen out of love with Gail. She was – and is – a wonderful woman, and neither of us had done anything wrong. Maybe it was because I had spent so much time on the business, or maybe it was some other reason, or maybe there was no reason at all. Whatever it was, I knew our marriage was over, and once I had accepted that I had to find a way to tell Gail.

It was one of the hardest conversations I've ever had – it was not as if she had done anything wrong, or that life at home was terrible; I had simply fallen out of love and had started to feel trapped. But once I had confessed how I felt, we sat down calmly and worked out how we would start to live apart. Initially we agreed to a trial separation, but within a few months we both accepted that divorce was inevitable.

Looking back on my divorce from Gail now, and comparing it to the contentious divorce I have recently been through with my second wife, I have so much respect for her and the way we handled things. It's also obvious to me now that meeting my second wife was partly the cause of my first divorce. Joanne McCue had been one of our nursing managers. Although I didn't realise it at the time, I was probably already falling in love with her. But back then I didn't make the connection.

Throughout our divorce, Gail and I put the kids first and she wasn't overcome by greed or suspicion or anything else. She said she had seen other couples get divorced acrimoniously and she wanted us to agree to do things differently.

She wanted us to buy the kids' birthday and Christmas presents together because she had seen other couples compete to buy the most expensive gifts. She wanted me to keep using a static caravan we had bought on Lake Windermere because she knew how much the kids loved staying there and going out on the water with me. And when it came to handovers she said to me: 'I'm not having you sitting outside and tooting the horn. You always come in and have a cup of coffee.'

Perhaps the most remarkable aspect of our divorce was when it came to filling in the custody arrangements. We simply wrote 'Both parents will always act in the best interest of the children at all times.' My solicitor thought the judge would never accept it, but instead we were praised for our attitude.

The financial settlement was fairly straightforward: I simply put shares in the company into her name, as married couples can transfer assets without paying tax, and then arranged for them to be sold. She got about £6 million and the house, and I was left with about 56% of the shares in the company. Gail and I are still good friends and it's very painful for me that my second divorce didn't work out that way too.

With four kids and two separate homes, childcare became a bit of a balancing act, especially as there were so many demands on me at work and I couldn't leave the office at short notice. Gail started looking around for a day nursery so that the youngest two could be looked after when she needed to be with the older two. We had difficulty finding a nursery with availability on the days we needed cover – especially somewhere that could look after Jennifer and Eve together. This made me think that perhaps Quality Care Homes could expand to start providing day care for the under-fives. The only problem I had was persuading the board that it was the right way to expand. They were reluctant: after all, their priority was the short-term value of our shares.

After a particularly frustrating board meeting, Michael Fallon, who was one of my more experienced directors, came to have a private chat with me. To my surprise, he told me he liked the idea of expanding into day care and wondered if he and I could do it as a separate venture. He said that he was willing to do most of the work if I could put up the cash.

He really couldn't have been a better partner for the venture – as a former education minister in the Thatcher government, Michael knew his way round legislation and red tape. We drew up an agreement that I would put up all the cash – in total it was around £2 million – and keep 90% of the company.

Michael (who later became the Minister for Business in the Coalition government) worked extremely hard, and Just Learning rapidly opened new centres, as well as acquiring facilities from other operators. The business grew very quickly and obviously caught some people's attention because in 1997 we received an offer from a company that wanted to buy us out for £12 million – a pretty good return on my investment. In the end, the sale didn't go through but it made Michael and I realise that we were happy to sell if we got the right price, and so we instructed agents to find us a buyer. It was done by the sealed-bid system and the last envelope we opened contained a stunning offer – £22 million!

Working with Michael on Just Learning reminded me how much more I enjoyed running a private business than a publicly listed one. Every time I had a clash with someone on the board, or they wanted me to adjust the dividend or appoint another director, I began to wonder if I really wanted to carry on running Quality Care Homes. I couldn't quite believe that I was actually considering selling the business I had started from scratch – the business I loved – but the time was starting to feel right for a fresh start. By now I had begun a relationship with Joanne McCue, whom I had promoted to become our director of nursing. I was head over heels in love with her. The idea of selling up and starting a new business with Joanne was incredibly appealing.

Early in 1997, the company was approached by an American firm that wanted to get a toehold in the British care-home market. They said they were interested in buying our freeholds. I wondered if this was the deal I had been looking for, but was unhappy about selling the freeholds separately from the operational side of things. As part of the negotiations, they found a partner to buy the operational business that would then pay rent to the company that bought the freeholds. The deal valued the business at a little over £46 million, of which £26 million was mine. Just over £6 million of that went into a trust for my children, meaning I received a cheque for a little over £19 million, which I quickly deposited into Northern Rock. Walking away from a company you started, a company you've fought for, is never easy, but I felt so positive about the future that I didn't look back: I was absolutely raring to start my next business.

With money in my account from the sale of both businesses, I didn't need a bank manager's approval to build my first health club, and after more than a decade of constructing care homes and day nurseries, I was able to start Bannatyne Fitness from a position of knowledge and experience – it was completely different from when I had risked everything on credit cards to start Quality Care Homes. Some things didn't change, however: I still kept tight control on our spending and wouldn't shell out for anything we didn't need – and that included an office. For the first few years, Bannatyne Fitness's head office was my dining-room table.

Between 1997 and 2005 we opened about four clubs a year. Most of those were built from scratch, but occasionally we'd acquire premises from other operators. As the business expanded, I started to promote the company's financial controller, a very able young guy called Nigel Armstrong.

Nigel tells me now that when I initially interviewed him I told him that he could end up running the business one day if he worked hard. I don't remember saying that, but it's exactly what has happened. Through a series of promotions Nigel became the Bannatyne Group's managing director, and he is now the chief executive. I gradually handed over the day-to-day running of the business to him and have now taken more of a back seat as the company's chairman. I am always at the end of a phone if Nigel needs me, and I am still in the office most weeks, but putting Nigel in charge has given me the time to make TV shows and write books. It has another advantage too: Nigel is much better at running the company than I am. I mean it. My skill is to get something off the ground and up and running. The truth is that I find operating a stable company a bit boring, as the challenges involved are very different.

The company went from strength to strength under Nigel's leadership, which allowed me to enjoy spending time with Joanne and our two kids, Emily and Tom, at a villa I'd bought in the south of France. Some of the very best times in my life have been spent there, mucking about in the pool with the kids, or just sitting on the terrace with a glass of wine.

And that's where I was at in 2006 when I was writing *Anyone Can Do It*. I was in a good place. I felt secure. I was incredibly happy and it really felt like the right time to look back and work out how a scruffy kid from Clydebank had got so lucky.

The publication of my autobiography wasn't the only significant thing that happened to me in 2006. In November of that year, I finally married Joanne. It had never been an issue that we weren't married – to be honest I think I had been too busy building Bannatyne Fitness for most of our relationship even to consider it. But in 2006 I was entering a new phase. I really felt that, after nearly 30 years in business, it was time to start enjoying the rewards. I was 57, I had the villa and I wanted to spend as much time there as I could. More than that, I realised I wanted to spend time there with Joanne and the kids: getting married felt right.

There's one other thing happened in 2006 that has continued to have a big impact on my life. The company got the opportunity to buy 24 health clubs from the Hilton hotel group. It turned out to be an incredibly significant acquisition for reasons that will become painfully apparent throughout the rest of this book. But I didn't know that then; all I knew was that I was deeply in love, enjoying my new TV career, and relishing the opportunities to get involved with lots of exciting media and charity events while Nigel looked after the business.

The view from 2006 was beautiful, the business equivalent of standing on the terrace of my villa in the south of France gazing at the Mediterranean and thinking how calm and gorgeous everything looked. But somewhere out at sea, beyond the horizon, a storm was brewing.

SIX

A Loan to Value?

The health clubs Bannatyne Fitness bought from Hilton were called LivingWell (Hilton still operate LivingWell clubs *within* their hotels – we bought all their stand-alone clubs). We negotiated a price of £92 million, based on profits of £12 million a year. This represented a very good deal for us – slightly less than eight times profits – but the deal was even sweeter because we estimated we could make improvements and efficiencies that would add another £3 million to the total.

Based on the lending deals on offer at the time, we calculated that our repayments on the loan we'd need to make the acquisition would be around £10 million a year. That meant a boost to our cash flow of £5 million a year after making the payments, plus a significant hike in the company's valuation. It's not hard to see why we were keen to do the deal.

Given that it was blindingly obvious to me and my

managing director that the deal was a smart move, it was frustrating that we found it difficult to get the lending. This was a year before the words 'subprime' and 'credit crunch' hit the headlines, and we were surprised that our usual banks wouldn't lend us the money.

'But we'll make an extra £5 million after interest and bank repayments. Every year. What's the problem?'

It felt like when I'd been trying to get a loan for the first care home: yet again I had a virtually guaranteed revenue but the banks we spoke to were worried about our gearing. They felt that our loan-to-value ratio was a little too close for comfort and borrowing £90 million would almost exactly double the level of debt in the company. They didn't seem to care that it would also boost our assets.

In the light of the banking crisis that started to make its presence felt on the front pages a year later, it's interesting that we were having such troubles in 2006. Banks have been reprimanded for their irresponsible lending, but they were certainly cautious with us. At some point during the negotiations I began to wonder whether it was less to do with the state of our business, and more to do with the state of theirs. On more than one occasion Nigel Armstrong – my MD – and I had conversations in which we said we didn't think they had the money to lend. I wonder now if the bankers already had some idea of what was to come.

At the time I didn't stop to think too much about all this, and in our determination to make the acquisition we carried on meeting with potential lenders. It was when we set up a meeting with Anglo Irish Bank that we finally had a breakthrough. Not only were they willing to lend, but they made us a very tempting offer: they wanted to lend us £180 million so we could pay off all our existing loans within Bannatyne Fitness (the hotels I own are a separate company with separate finance) and only borrow from them. Another benefit was that they were offering us a very good rate – 1.65% above the interbank lending rate known as LIBOR, which was a significantly lower rate than our existing loans. So not only would we be able to buy those LivingWell clubs, but the low interest rate meant we could borrow twice as much money for only a modest increase in our monthly repayments. We were extremely happy to accept the offer.

Interestingly, when we met with Allied Irish Bank about the transfer of some of our existing loans from them to Anglo Irish, one of the Allied managers said to us, 'I don't know how they can lend you this money when we can't; they are punching way above their weight.' I didn't think too much of it at the time.

Given how significant this loan has turned out to be for the company, I should probably set out the terms of the agreement. Anglo Irish lent us £180 million at a rate pegged to LIBOR. The paperwork ran to a couple of hundred pages, and contained in that document were some covenants – a banking term for special conditions that protect the bank in the event that the company they're lending to runs into trouble – that all seemed fairly standard. However, two of them turned out to be very significant: one was that our loan-to-value ratio – the amount of debt the company could have in relation to its value – could not rise above 58%, and the other was that our profits had to stay above the level we were projecting. If either of those covenants were broken,

Anglo Irish would be entitled to impose a monitoring fee of about £100,000 a month on Bannatyne Fitness, and switch the loan to a higher interest rate. They would also have the right to call in the entire loan if they wanted to. Way back in 2006 we didn't anticipate that either of those covenants posed even a minor risk; if we did momentarily find ourselves in breach, we were pretty sure we'd be the only ones who would know about it, as we had never heard of a bank monitoring a business that closely.

There is one other significant aspect of the loan arrangement I should mention: it was fixed for ten years. At the end of that period – which falls on 8 August 2016, a date seared into my brain for reasons that will become obvious – Anglo Irish can call in the loan, that is ask for any outstanding money to be repaid. We had no problem with this at all – after ten years we assumed we would shop around for the best deal anyway. And besides, we estimated we would repay so much of the debt that by 2016, we'd only need to borrow £90 million. It never occurred to us – not for one second – that the banks could run out of money and that they might not have £90 million to lend in 2016.

But I'm getting ahead of myself.

SEVEN

Growing the Business

The reason why Bannatyne Fitness had loans from several different lenders before the Anglo Irish deal was that back in the early days of the business, when we'd been expanding rapidly, I had run up against the barrier of the banks' loan-to-value requirements. I'd had cash in the bank from the sale of Just Learning that I wanted to use to secure the lending, but there was no point putting that cash into the existing company because if we ever defaulted on those loans, I was just handing my cash to the lender. Instead, I incorporated Bannatyne Fitness 2, Bannatyne Fitness 3 and Bannatyne Fitness 4, and put a parcel of money into each of them so that each company could take out loans independently of the others.

Now that we just had one lender, I wanted to do what's known as a 'hive-up' and transfer the assets of all the companies into Bannatyne Fitness. Thanks to a clause in our loan agreement with Anglo Irish, we were allowed to take a year's payment holiday during the ten-year loan period. So, shortly after the acquisition, we decided to make full use of that clause; instead of making repayments of £10 million, we used that money to buy assets from Bannatyne Fitness 2, 3 and 4. At the end of the hive-up, there was around £3 million left over that I deposited in a bank account – just in case I ever needed it for a rainy day.

One of the most dangerous things you can do in business is to think that you know it all. There is no such thing as 'too experienced'. It's one of the reasons I still get a massive kick out of making *Dragons' Den* – not only do I learn from the other dragons about their sectors and their businesses, but I also learn from the entrepreneurs who ask us for investment (even if it's mainly what *not* to do!). Nevertheless, I was still a little surprised that I learned quite so much about how to run a health club from our acquisition of the LivingWell clubs.

My team immediately set about making changes to the new clubs, rebranding them, standardising their membership tiers, bringing in new management oversight and getting tough on late payers and non-payers. It didn't take long for us to notice a rapid widening in our profit margin.

For the first few months after the LivingWell acquisition, we analysed the figures from the new clubs incredibly closely. To our surprise we discovered something we really hadn't been expecting: the spas in our new clubs made a profit. Quite a big one. £40,000 to £60,000 a year in most cases.

By this stage, I had been operating health clubs for almost exactly a decade and I had never come across spas making significant amounts of money. I had always viewed them as the sort of add-on that encouraged some people – almost all of them women – to take out a health-club membership. They were valuable in attracting members, but on their own they didn't make a profit. Or at least that's what I'd always thought.

Bannatyne Fitness owned almost exactly 60 clubs. If we put a spa in every club, and each made a profit of £50,000, that would increase our annual bottom line by £3 million a year. Unsurprisingly, we suddenly became very interested in working out why the LivingWell spas were making a profit when other health-club spas were barely breaking even, and then rolling them out to as many of our existing clubs as possible.

We discovered that the reason why Hilton had made a profit on the LivingWell spas was because they had a call centre to handle the bookings. The call centre could see the availability of all the treatment rooms and all the therapists, which made bookings very efficient. But more importantly, it meant that the individual spas didn't each have to employ someone to take the bookings. Even in the spas where the therapists were taking the bookings themselves, the centralised system freed them up to offer more treatments.

We appointed a new spa director to oversee the expansion of that side of the business, and poached a guy named Justin Musgrove from Center Parcs where he had been in charge of their spa services. With someone on the team who knew which treatments were the most in demand, and which were the most profitable, our spa expansion became a major driver of our growth in profits.

We started with our biggest clubs, that is those with the

most members. If they already had spas, we improved and expanded them, and where necessary we built extensions for the treatment rooms. We now have spas in 32 out of our 61 clubs, but it's unlikely that we'll roll them out to every single club as there seems to be a resistance level around the 2,000-member mark. If we go below that level, we don't get the return we want (although our Mansfield club bucks this trend, so there's no hard-and-fast rule).

As well as selling manicures and massages to members who were coming into our health clubs already, we started selling spa packages to non-members. They could use our pools, steam rooms and saunas whenever they had a treatment, and the sales of day spa packages have been phenomenal. In an age when everyone is tightening their belts, a spa treatment is considered an affordable treat. We quickly brought in vouchers, making a Bannatyne Spa day a really easy gift to give. We then started to sell a lot of our spa days through third parties like Red Letter Days and Buy-a-Gift; although they take around 25% in commission, it works out cheaper for us than advertising – and it's more targeted.

The spa business has also had a positive impact on one of my other businesses, Bannatyne Hotels Ltd. I opened my first hotel in the late 1990s when my future wife Joanne and I were actively looking for places for me to invest my money. We discovered that a rundown hotel in the centre of Darlington had come up for sale. It was a beautiful Georgian building with 24 bedrooms. It had clearly been very grand at one point but had suffered from years of neglect and underinvestment. Joanne had a long-held ambition to open what she called 'a restaurant with rooms' and so I bought it and she pretty much took charge of the renovations. At the time I was focused on getting the health clubs up and running, so I was happy to take a back seat and let her open her dream business.

She had ambitions for the Grange Hotel to rival Raymond Blanc's Manoir, which is one of the finest restaurants in the country. People go there for the food, then stay over because they are too full to move very far (or too drunk to drive). Although the food in the Grange was probably the best in the north-east, and the rooms were gorgeous, there just weren't enough customers in the area who were prepared to pay for haute cuisine. So I stepped in and put a rescue plan in place.

My plan was to put the focus on it being a hotel that just happened to have a restaurant. This made sense as we had a waiting list for bedrooms but an empty dining room, so I instructed an architect to build an extension. The extra rooms enabled me to massively increase the income without massively increasing staff costs. After all, a hotel with 40 rooms still only needs one restaurant, one bar and one reception. It was such a success that we subsequently built a second extension, taking us to 60 rooms, which meant we were big enough to attract more wedding bookings – a major source of income for a hotel like the Grange.

I also made changes to the restaurant. There just wasn't enough demand for fine dining in Darlington, so I worked with the chef to alter the menu: essentially simpler meals and bigger portions. This was very successful and had an immediate impact on our profits.

My second hotel was completely different. We had some spare land next to our Durham health club and, knowing that accommodation often got booked up in Durham, we thought a hotel in the area would do well. The model was more along the lines of a Travelodge or a Premier Inn, only we would have one major advantage over those two companies – our hotel in Durham wouldn't need a reception, which meant it wouldn't be paying receptionists' salaries. In fact there was a lot the Durham hotel wouldn't need, including a restaurant, because all those facilities would be offered by the health club next door. Customers would pick up their keys from the club and use the café in the club for breakfast. And, of course, hotel guests could also make use of all the club's facilities. There was a time when we planned to roll out a chain of these hotels wherever we had appropriate plots of land next to our clubs, but it's been one of the many ideas we've had to put on hold since lending dried up.

However, we did make two more acquisitions. In 2007 we were informed that the Beauport Park Hotel next to our health club in Hastings – the club is actually in the grounds of the hotel – had been put up for sale, and as this gave us the chance to offer the club's facilities to hotel guests, it was obviously a very good fit for us. We made the usual enquiries, had a look at the figures and decided to put in an offer, which was successful.

Then in 2010 we got a call from liquidators who were looking to sell a hotel in Shepton Mallet. Charlton House already had a spa, and seemed a very good fit with our portfolio, so we made the acquisition. By this point, we were so good at operating spas that we knew several ways to increase the profits at both hotels.

EIGHT

How to Run a Hotel

Beauport Park is a beautiful country house hotel set in 37 acres of land. It's a lovely building in a fantastic setting, but at the time I acquired it its interior had become dated and neglected – it was the kind of place you took your grandmother for Sunday lunch rather than your girlfriend for a weekend away. It was easy to see how a refurbishment would transform the clientele.

We set about bringing the design into the 21st century and built an extension to increase the number of rooms. The place was rebranded as the Bannatyne Spa Hotel and almost overnight the atmosphere and the clientele changed. That had an immediate impact on the finances. In the long term, we think there are also opportunities to make additional profits if we develop those 37 acres.

Charlton House is possibly an even nicer hotel. Just outside Shepton Mallet in Somerset, it's an incredible building in a stunning part of the country, but the previous owners hadn't been able make it pay. I felt sure we'd be able to find a way, so when a sales agent approached us to see if we were interested, I immediately booked myself a room.

I find it fascinating how one person – or one company – can make a success of the same business where another has failed. I've watched Theo Paphitis become an expert in buying struggling retailers and turning them around. Peter Jones is now doing the same thing with his acquisition of the camera chain Jessops. Just as Theo can walk into a shop and instantly assess what the owner has got wrong about displays, lighting, price points and layout, I can do the same with hotels.

The main thing I was looking out for when I went to see Charlton House was how we could increase the number of bedrooms for the smallest possible cost. The day-to-day cost of adding rooms is incremental – a bit of extra laundry and cleaning – which means the income you get from them is almost entirely profit.

I checked in, had a drink in the bar, ate in the restaurant and the next morning I was given a tour. I was shown a room behind reception that had about six desks in it.

'Whose office is this?' I asked.

'Well that's the manager's desk, that's the chef's desk, that desk is used by the gardener –'

'Wait. The *gardener* has a desk? Why?'

It was one of those classic situations where a business was doing something for the sole reason that they had always been doing it. I'd never heard of a chef needing a dedicated desk, let alone a gardener. I immediately saw that it would be possible to incorporate the manager's desk into the reception area, and knew I had found an extra bedroom. In my head I was thinking '£179 a night, 75% occupancy rate, turnover of £50,000 a year.'

Charlton House already had a small spa, so I was pretty sure we'd be able to overhaul its spa operations. As it was a weekend and wedding hotel rather than a city-centre business hotel, there was hardly any demand for single rooms and Charlton House had a single room that was rarely let out. We saw another opportunity: it was big enough to put a double bed in, so we did that and started marketing it as the 'tiny double'. This meant guests were under no illusions about its size, and it had the added bonus of attracting couples who might not have otherwise been able to afford to stay, and of course they still booked meals and spa treatments. That was another boost to turnover.

We also looked at the grounds, which were – and are – beautiful, and saw a couple of other ways to boost income. The first was to improve the wedding service, since it was a wonderful location to get married in, and the second was to install a log cabin – the ultimate in luxury and privacy for a getaway. It would be a double room we could charge a premium for.

Of course there are other benefits when a company like ours takes over a business like Charlton House. As I mentioned earlier, since our acquisition of LivingWell we have call centres to take bookings. You can arrange your accommodation and spa treatments at the same time; we have a centralised payroll, fantastic management skills, and as a large business we have bargaining power with external contractors such as breweries which helps save on costs.

With all this added together, it was easy to see how we could make Charlton House profitable again.

Valuing a business is usually straightforward as it's commonly just a standard multiple of profits. In the hotel industry, that multiple is ten. The profits for Charlton House were £250,000, therefore its price should have been £2.5 million. But the liquidators wanted £4 million for it. We thought that was way too high, but we estimated that we could instantly make changes that would boost the profits, meaning it was worth £3 million to us (that was also the price we thought it would fetch if it was converted back into a private house). We put in a bid for £3 million but it was rejected: the liquidators were holding out for £4 million.

'OK,' I said, 'see if you can get someone to offer you more.'

They were no doubt thinking that a buyer would visit the property and be so bowled over by it – it really is stunning – that they would get excited and offer over the odds. But buying a business isn't like buying a house, where you might pay a premium for a pretty garden or a top location: it doesn't matter what a business is worth to someone else, only what it's worth to you. And we knew our figure was £3 million.

As it turned out, no one else bid more than we did and a month later we got a call asking if we still wanted to proceed. We did the deal, started making changes and soon the profits started to rise.

I had hoped to open a chain of spa hotels like Beauport Park and Charlton House, but events, and the economy, have put those plans on hold. It's disappointing, but I just can't be sentimental about it any more – I've been doing this for a long time now, and experience has taught me that sometimes things go to plan, and other times they don't. The secret to staying solvent is to always deal with how things are, rather than how you want them to be.

Charlton House is the kind of place you have to pinch yourself about owning. It's no surprise to me that it's incredibly popular for weddings, although I have to say that might also have something to do with the fact that we have a fantastic wedding and events manager there – my daughter Hollie. She studied Events Management at university and after graduating worked at a venue in the City of London, where she became the manager. I didn't think she'd ever come and work with me; in fact, as children, none of my daughters from my first marriage expressed a great enthusiasm for working for the company. However, as they grew up they started to understand what it means to have a family business, and over the past few years that's exactly what it has become. I've heard loads of entrepreneurs refer to their businesses as 'like having another child' but I see now that the Bannatyne Group hasn't just been important to me, it's been meaningful to them too. They've grown up with it, it's got their name over the door, they see the jobs we create and the money we raise for charity and they are all extremely passionate about its continued success. I'm enormously proud that three of my daughters are now on the payroll.

After a spell working for the company in Manchester, Hollie took on the events role at Charlton House and she has done an amazing job – not just for the countless brides and grooms, but for our accounts too. She had not been in the job very long when she came to me and said she'd looked at how we billed for weddings and knew a way to add around £3,000 profit to every wedding.

'For most weddings, we put a marquee in the grounds, and that costs us £3,000 which obviously we pass on to the client,' she said. 'I've looked at the bookings, and there are times on a Sunday when there are only a few people having dinner in the restaurant. I'm pretty sure most brides would pay £3,000 for exclusive use of the restaurant.'

She was right: we could save £3,000 on our costs, and the only loss of revenue was a few covers in the restaurant. Chip off the old block.

I know I'm not the only one happy with Hollie's work, because if you go on TripAdvisor, you'll see plenty of comments from guests who are full of praise for her. And as her name badge doesn't have her surname on it, I know they're judging her on her work and not on who her dad is.

Talking of TripAdvisor, it was only when we bought Charlton House that I fully understood the power this site has over the travel industry. Most people will look at a hotel online before they book, and a large percentage of them will have looked at TripAdvisor, which collects reviews and has forums for discussion. Of course this kind of online community is a pretty recent development in the industry – when I first started out in business, a couple of lines in an old-fashioned visitors' book were the most feedback any hotel was likely to get, and that feedback wasn't accessible to the general public.

There's a lot to be said for being able to hear the honest, uncensored opinions of your clientele. A lot of customers don't feel comfortable giving that kind of feedback directly to a member of staff, but the things they have to say can draw attention to issues which we might have overlooked ourselves.

That said, our experiences with online feedback certainly haven't been entirely positive. It's a system which is open to abuse. TripAdvisor and sites like it use a five-star system which means that the odd one-star review can really drag down the average and give a false impression of your establishment. It's also possible for anyone at all to leave a review – there are no checks in place to verify that people have actually stayed at the hotel they are criticising (or indeed praising). There have been numerous instances of B&B owners in small towns using specially created email accounts to slate their rivals and to give themselves five stars.

We've had more than a few instances of abuse of this kind ourselves but there was one time in particular which made me absolutely furious. I read a one-star review of Charlton House one morning and just knew it was someone trying it on because it mentioned that the hotel is on a busy road, which it isn't. But I still called up the team there and asked them what they thought had gone wrong with this guest. They told me that she was just an extremely awkward customer. She had checked in on a Sunday, our cheapest night, and gone for a meal with her husband in the restaurant. They proceeded to complain about every single course – but only after they'd eaten three quarters of it! In the morning when she checked out she told the reception staff that the night porter had agreed she could have a discount because they had been disturbed by the (non-existent) road noise.

This would have been par for the course – there will

always be a few people whom it's impossible to please – had it not been for the fact that she actually worked for a PR firm that was in the process of bidding for the Charlton House account! She wanted to use her TripAdvisor review to show how she thought we could improve our customer relations!

I'm sure you can imagine how angry I was when I found out. It was so breathtakingly unprofessional that I felt completely justified in naming her and her company on Twitter. The only way to deal with bullies is to stand up to them.

We now have an in-house legal team working at our head office in Darlington that includes my daughter Jennifer. It's one of her jobs to check TripAdvisor on a daily basis and if she sees anything defamatory or libellous, we make sure we respond immediately: you can't let that kind of thing go unchallenged.

NINE

Let's Tweet About It

Online reviews have had a big impact on almost every industry – that's simply a reality of modern business. Whether they want to buy a book or hire a plumber, the first thing most people do nowadays is go online, search, then read the reviews. Retailers no longer need to employ sales teams who know absolutely every product on the market, because most of their customers can compare a much bigger range online. And instead of just getting one person's point of view, you get several.

Although this encourages some people to complain about minor irritations in a way they wouldn't have bothered to before the internet, online review sites are great for consumers. And ultimately, what's good for consumers has to be good for business – if a bad review helps you make a better product or offer a better service, then in the long term you'll have more happy customers. I sometimes wonder how business – and society – functioned before the internet.

When I wrote *Anyone Can Do It* in 2006, Twitter hadn't been invented, and yet now I can't imagine my life without it. I find it the best way to get to know my customers and to respond to their frustrations and suggestions. It took me a while to cotton on to it, and I actually only started using it after I read an article in a paper that mentioned I'd had dinner at the Ivy with Peter Jones and James Caan. I hadn't been at the Ivy, so I called the journalist who'd written the article and asked why he thought I had.

'You tweeted about it.'

'But I'm not on Twitter.'

'Are you sure?'

So I went on Twitter and sure enough, there I was. Or, more accurately, there was someone pretending to be me. I guess I should be glad that he wasn't using the account to say horrible things about my friends and colleagues, but in a way it seemed even stranger that my impostor was just using the account to tweet mundane things such as where I was having dinner, or when I was having meetings.

It turned out to be a teenage boy who was living out some kind of fantasy by pretending to be me. The only way to prove who was the real me was to join Twitter myself. Not long afterwards, the dragons were all due to appear on the Jonathan Ross show, but I was in France at the time and didn't want to leave my family so the other four went on without me. I tweeted a message to Jonathan but I didn't get a reply, so I tweeted again, saying 'You think this is a fake account, don't you?' He tweeted back one word: 'Yeah.' So I took a photo of myself and sent it to him. Once he realised I was genuine, so did lots of other people. I soon got that little blue tick beside my name and my number of followers started to increase. There are now over 600,000 people who follow me.

As far as I'm concerned Twitter is both good for pleasure and great for business. It's a fun way to talk to people about *Britain's Got Talent* or something in the news, but it's also a brilliant way for our health-club members – and sometimes our staff – to get in touch if there's something they think I need to know about. Most of the time, people just want to tell me how much they've enjoyed their spa day, or how good the service they received at one of our clubs was.

Occasionally, of course, people use it to complain, but that's OK with me, so long as they can back it up with times, dates, names and maybe even photos. Sometimes I'll get a tweet saying something like, 'The showers at our club have been cold for a week.' So I'll reply and say, 'Give me a clue, which club is it?' When I get the information, I'll contact my estates director, Steve Hancock, who'll tell me that the showers have actually only been cold for a day or two and that they're scheduled to be fixed by the morning. I can then tweet that information back to the complainer, who's usually very happy that something is getting sorted so quickly.

Once, a woman got in touch to say that we had cancelled two spa treatments and her voucher was now out of date. I investigated, and it turned out that we had let her down, so we immediately extended her voucher period by six months. Mostly, people only get in touch with real issues, but some people just want to shoot their mouths off. One guy recently ranted that my staff couldn't organise a piss-up in a brewery, so I got straight back to him and told him that no one talks about my staff like that: he could either apologise immediately or we'd revoke his membership. He said sorry very quickly after that.

At least he had the courage to use his real name: it's the people who hide behind false identities and throw insults without any justification that I have no time for. They're complete cowards, and I have no problem retweeting their accusations to my followers so that half a million people can know how petty and spiteful they are.

Sometimes, though, the accusations and threats have been so serious that I've had to go to the police. In 2011, I received this on Twitter:

> Dear Dragon. My name is Yuri Vasilyev and I'm looking for a £35,000 investment to stop us hurting your Hollie Bannatyne. We will bring hurt and pain into your life.

Then, a bit later, I was sent this:

> We are watching her. She is very attractive. Want photos? Tweet using the hashtag #4money to confirm payment will be made.

Even though I was pretty sure Hollie wasn't in any danger, the need I feel to protect my children is immense. If someone thinks it's a game to threaten my family, then they're going to have to learn to play by my rules. The first thing I did was employ a private security firm to keep an eye on Hollie. I decided not to tell her though, as I thought it might alarm her unnecessarily. The next thing I did was tweet this:

I offer £25,000 reward for the capture of the coward who calls himself @YuriVasilyev_ Double if his arms are broken first

I also got the police involved and they asked me to delete the tweet as it was inciting people to commit an act of violence. That seemed reasonable, so I posted the following:

OK £30,000 reward for info leading to his arrest

Twitter might allow cowards to act spitefully, but it also gives people a chance to come together, and there were a few who took up the challenge and were determined to track him down. It's one of the reasons why I love it so much: with one tweet you can form an online army.

A couple of people traced the blackmailer's IP address to an internet café in Moscow, and it turned out to be the same IP address used by a guy who ran a website selling cameras. The people told me who they thought he was and so I sent him an email telling him I knew his identity. I waited for his reply.

Hollie was a bit worried but I think it helped that at the time she was staying with her sister Abigail and my son-in-law Anthony, who is a 6'4" rugby player. Anthony phoned me at one point during this saga and said 'Duncan, do you think I should call the police? There's somebody outside the house.' I told him not to worry because it was the security team I had hired. So Anthony went outside and asked them in for a cup of tea!

Knowing that Hollie was being taken care of meant I only

had to worry about my Russian troll. He had replied to my email and insisted that Hollie was going to get hurt. 'We will bring pain and fear,' he wrote. 'We are the men of Belarus. We do not give up. We will stand tall. You should have paid. £35,000 to stop it. Contact us to pay. We are watching. Expect us. We are the men of Belarus.'

So I wrote back and said, 'Listen arsehole, you live in Moscow not Belarus, you're using an internet café, your real name is —— and you sell cameras for a living.' Then I added: 'I'm looking at you, I'm going to get you and break your legs and break your arms. Look over your shoulder.'

Funnily enough, I never heard another thing from him.

That's the only truly horrible experience I've ever had with Twitter. Most people just want to say how much they enjoyed visiting one of my hotels, or how they were inspired by one of my books – that stuff is brilliant to hear and I'm grateful to be able to have that kind of contact with people. Inevitably, there are a few people out there who use it to have a go, people who say I'm just showing off because I'm wealthy! Most of the time I just let it go but sometimes I can't resist responding. I asked one guy how old he was and he said he was 28. I tweeted back and said he was a damn sight wealthier than I was at 28 because I didn't even have a bank account at that age. Anyone who's under 30 and has a bank account is ahead of where I was at their age. If they're jealous of the money I've earned they'd be better off putting their energy into earning some themselves than tweeting pointless insults.

The thing is, I never get abuse face to face. It's only when they're hiding behind fake identities or coded usernames that people have a go. They're keyboard warriors. Which makes them cowards, and it's impossible to be scared of cowards. I have no problem posting photos of my kids, or letting people know where I am on Twitter, because I know that the trolls can't stand real life.

Twitter is also a powerful promotional tool. With over half a million followers, it's possible to let a lot of people know when we've got a special offer for spa days, or when a new book comes out. I can tweet about a book and a couple of hours later I'll see a spike in its ranking on Amazon.

Twitter is also great for raising the profile of – and money for – some of the charities I'm involved with. I did a skydive a couple of years ago to raise money for Pilgrim Bandits, a charity that helps injured soldiers (more about them later). I asked people if they wanted to come along. More than 40 people did, and they all raised sponsorship. Hollie also organised a dinner and auction at Charlton House for Pilgrim Bandits, and with some help from Twitter we sold two tables' worth of seats within a few hours. It's just one of the many reasons that I love Twitter.

TEN

Den of Iniquity

Of course, one of the main reasons I have 600,000 followers on Twitter is because I've been on TV quite a lot in the past decade. I think it's fair to say that when we started filming *Dragons' Den* in 2004, none of us thought it would still be going after 11 series. Possibly even more surprising is that there are only two people who have worked on all those series – either in front of or behind the camera – and that's me and Peter Jones.

I've never asked him, but I'm pretty sure Peter would agree that we saw ourselves as rivals right from the start; however, I also hope he'd agree that we have since become very good friends. If you look at the dragons on the first series – me, Peter, Doug Richard, Rachel Elnaugh and Simon Woodroffe – it would be quite easy to predict that there would be a bit of rivalry between us. Simon (the founder of Yo! Sushi) is a very laid-back guy, and Doug (a technology investor) comes under the heading of intellectual and aloof. Peter and I were more along the lines of the typical competitive alpha male.

I don't know how much of this the producers sensed, but very early on in filming there was a pitch that highlighted the tension between us and so it was edited and packaged into the very first episode. It cemented the rivalry for a few years to come. The pitch had been for Umbrolly, a company that had plans to put umbrella-vending machines in Tube stations. The founder, a very impressive young businessman called Charles Ejogo, was looking for £150,000 and I thought both he and his company could be extremely successful. So did Peter and Doug, and all three of us made offers. At some point in the negotiations, Peter offered Charles £75,000 for a 22% stake, and I agreed to match it, but Charles wasn't prepared to give up 44% of his company. Doug then offered him the entire £150,000 and asked Charles to make him an offer on the percentage. He suggested 35%, but Doug turned him down.

It was at this point that the tension between Peter and I went off the scale. Peter offered to take just 20%, but when Charles asked me to match it, I said I was sticking at 22% – the opportunity hadn't changed, so I didn't see why my offer should. Charles took the deal at 42%, but as soon as he left the Den, Peter started fuming. 'I've been had,' he said, and the microphone picked him up calling me a 'sly little shit'. It obviously made for fantastic TV, but in truth a lot of that animosity was real. So much so that I asked Charles to come back into the Den and agreed to only take 20%, as it was clear that to leave the deal as it was would make Peter a seriously unenthusiastic investor.

Peter thought I had made him look silly on the 22% thing. I think he saw it as a threat to his business acumen, and it took him a while to forgive me. Things stayed cool between us for a long time afterwards. It's nearly ten years since we first started working together, and in that time I think Peter and I have somehow grown up together. I now see him for what he is – an incredibly hard-working and successful entrepreneur who is doing fantastic work sponsoring academy schools where he's encouraging the next generation of entrepreneurs.

Although Peter and I didn't always get on, I think we always respected each other. We don't often invest together because we are naturally drawn to different products and businesses – it's one of the reasons why the *Dragons' Den* format is so successful. But the one thing Peter and I definitely have in common is that we both have large families (I've got six kids, he's got five). So when an entrepreneur comes into the Den with a product that helps, or protects, or encourages children in some way, Peter and I often find ourselves making competing offers. Very occasionally – just four times since the 22% row – we have ended up investing together. One of those opportunities came in series three, and it made Peter and me realise, probably for the first time, that we had more in common than we'd thought.

Autosafe was a seat-belt adapter that made seat belts much safer for children to use. It had been invented and developed by a lovely man called Peter Sesay. He didn't give the most accomplished pitch, but Peter and I shared the view that if Autosafe saved just one child's life then it would be the best investment we ever made. Very tragically, Peter Sesay was diagnosed with cancer not long after we made the investment, and he died before he had a chance to make Autosafe a success. I attended his funeral along with Peter Jones, and in the months that followed, when we bought out his widow's share of the company, Peter and I realised that the differences between us were pretty insignificant. You can't work with someone as long as we have if you don't respect each other, and out of that respect has come a real and valuable friendship.

I'm slightly surprised that Peter still does *Dragons' Den*. Of all of us he is the most financially successful and has probably had the most TV work outside the Den. But even though he's making a show based on Gordon Ramsay's *Kitchen Nightmares* for American TV, he still says yes to another year as a dragon.

None of us have ongoing contracts to stay with the show, and some years we don't even know if there will be another series. Even if another series has been confirmed, we still don't know if we'll be asked to return. The dragons who leave usually do so because they want to concentrate on other projects, but there have been occasions where the producers haven't invited people back. Contrary to what viewers think, that's not based on personalities or whether or not they have enough women or the right racial mix. I don't think there's an exact formula, but one of the things the producers are always looking for is dragons who actually invest. If a dragon goes right through a series without making an investment (it has happened), the producers will look to replace him or her: it just doesn't make good television if someone isn't prepared to embrace the reason for the show's existence – which is to back brilliant new businesses.

After the panel had been through a few changes, the

producers realised that replacing a couple of the dragons every now and then kept things fresh, so I am quite surprised that they have always asked me and Peter back. Perhaps they're hoping for another 22% moment. Or perhaps they have research data that shows we're popular. I really have no idea, I just know that so far I've always been very happy to say yes, and presumably so has Peter.

The contract is always the same – as is the fee, which has been £950 a day since the beginning – and we guarantee to make ourselves available for specified filming dates. We also have to pass a medical for insurance purposes, but as far as I know the BBC doesn't audit our finances to make sure we have the funds available to invest. However, if – as happened to Rachel Elnaugh when her business Red Letter Days got into trouble – there are lots of headlines about your business empire crumbling, I suppose it's unlikely you'd be asked to do another series.

Every line-up has its own dynamic, and when Theo Paphitis replaced Simon Woodroffe in series two, it was clear that Peter and Theo were very good mates. It didn't help that they sat next to each other in the Den, and they became quite a double act. I wasn't surprised that the producers split them up like naughty schoolboys for the third series.

I think the line-up that worked best was probably that of series three – me, Peter, Theo, Richard Farleigh and Deborah Meaden. I was quite shocked when Richard wasn't asked back because I thought he was a great investor, as well as a good mate, but my first impression of his replacement – James Caan – was that he would also be great for the Den. I went to meet James before we started filming and thought he was a really nice guy, well-educated and soft-spoken. I hadn't heard of him, but then I hadn't heard of Deborah before she joined the series either. It didn't stop me investing with him, though; in fact, I made my best-ever investment (and possibly the Den's best-ever investment) with James – Electro Expo Ltd, an electrical components manufacturer.

Like Theo and Peter, James was a smoker. And when we had a break in filming, they could all usually be found in the car park at Pinewood having a cigarette. The three of them – and Deborah – are much closer in age (I'm 17 years older than Peter) and there was a time when it really felt like they'd formed themselves into a little clique, especially after Theo and Deborah made a string of investments together. It wasn't nice to be on the outside of it, but when they went for a smoke I caught up on emails or had a cup of tea with the crew. I really didn't mind that much.

My relationship with James changed as we made investments together. After the success of Electro Expo we invested in a company called Magnamole that had been started by an entrepreneur called Sharon Wright. Sharon's invention made it easier to install electrical cabling, and there was an obvious advantage to be gained by rolling Sharon's company into Electro Expo.

When two dragons invest together, we usually agree at the studio which one of us will take the lead on the investment. There's no point in both of us doing due diligence or both of us drawing up contracts. With Magnamole, James and I agreed that I would lead the investment. I did the investigations and had my lawyer draw up the paperwork, and a few months after Sharon had been in the Den, we all met up at James's office in London to sign the documents.

Sharon was happy to sign but James refused, saying it wasn't a viable contract. He couldn't explain what the problem was in a way that I could understand, so I told him that if we didn't all sign it, it would only take more time and more money to sort it out. 'You're here, I'm here, Sharon's here, let's just sign it and be done with it,' I said.

James then pulled out a contract from his desk drawer and the upshot is that – because we trusted him – Sharon and I both signed James's contract. Without reading it properly, I should add. Unfortunately, it wasn't long before Sharon told me she was unhappy with the deal because James's investment was structured as if it was a loan. She also said that his company was trying to charge her company a management fee. I was really shocked – it was far too complicated an arrangement for a relatively small company like Sharon's. I felt caught in the middle, but I had signed it too so I didn't think there was anything I could do about it.

There were other investments James and I made together that made me realise we had different – and probably incompatible – criteria as investors, and this was in part because James was registered a 'non-dom' (i.e. not domiciled in the UK) for tax purposes. I remember a situation where he wanted to take dividends but I didn't see the point as I'd have to pay 40% tax on them: from my point of view it made sense to leave the money in the company.

Outside of the Den, James ran a private equity company and one of the ventures he backed was a chain of low cost gyms. It just struck me as profoundly wrong that one business will pay more in earnings than another business operating in the same industry if the owner has non-dom status. At the time I wrote a weekly column for the *Daily Telegraph*, and I used it to call on the government to change the law for non-doms. I felt that most people assumed non-doms were only allowed to spend a certain number of days a year in the country, not to live as essentially permanent residents. I thought that if readers understood more about non-doms, they'd be as angry as I was. I used the example of James and his Nuyuu gym – which had opened a branch a few hundred yards from our Livingstone club – to highlight the unfairness.

When we gathered at Pinewood a few months later for the start of another series of *Dragons' Den*, James refused to shake my hand. After that, we filmed the entire series without saying a word to each other.

ELEVEN

Musical Chairs

It wasn't a big surprise when James announced that he wouldn't be making a fifth series. He released a statement saying he was going to concentrate on his business, but filming can't have been much fun for him – by the end of his fourth series, none of the other dragons seemed to be close to him anymore. What was a surprise, however, was the dragon who replaced him: Hilary Devey.

The producers asked if I would do a screen test with one of the potential new dragons, and as I was available I was happy to help out. I went along, met Hilary, and then we sat and interrogated a couple of people on the production team who were pretending to have brilliant businesses in need of investment. Having taken part in the screen test, I have to admit I was quite surprised that they appointed Hilary. I had two reservations about her: the first was that I didn't think she asked particularly good questions, and the second was that I didn't think she would be physically able to take the long, hectic days on set – she was still recovering from a stroke at the time.

But the producers knew what they were doing – making good TV – and Hilary certainly got people talking about *Dragons' Den* again. That's no mean feat for a show starting its ninth series. She was – and is – a quirky customer who comes out with some peculiar phrases ('You make my foot itch!') and of course she has remarkable taste in fashion. However, she took her investing very seriously and took good care of the companies she put her money into.

Sadly, I was proved right about Hilary's health, and there were a couple of mornings where she just wasn't well enough to be on set. And in series ten in 2012, we had to film an entire episode without her; the show was broadcast with just four dragons.

The tenth series was the first to be filmed in Salford as part of the BBC's commitment to move a lot of their programme-making out of London. Millions were spent on building MediaCityUK at Salford Quays in Manchester and we now make the show in some of the most sophisticated studios in the world.

Over the 11 series, the Den has actually changed its location several times. For the first couple of series we filmed on location in disused warehouses in different parts of London, but there were often problems with access and noise, and eventually the decision was made to build a fake den inside Pinewood Studios. This had several practical advantages (easier parking, better catering) and it also meant the fake walls could be moved so that entrepreneurs could bring in really big prototypes for us to look at. The move to Salford was just another change and I really don't mind where the show is filmed. That said, of all the dragons, I've been the happiest with the move and that's probably because I'm the only one who lives in the north.

One of the major changes when we started filming in Salford was that instead of going home to our separate houses (as we did when we were at Pinewood), we all stayed in the same hotel. Four of us would also have dinner together – Hilary was never in a position to join us – and as a result we bonded more than we had done before. We almost always eat at the same restaurant, San Carlos. They take very good care of us and we spend an awful lot of money there. We usually have a couple of bottles of wine – Peter always orders it, and he likes *expensive* wine – and we play spoof to decide who foots the bill, which can sometimes be several hundred pounds. For a while it often seemed to be Deborah who ended up paying more than the rest of us. Sometimes friends and partners join us, but we'll only let them play spoof if they can afford to lose.

For the 11th series – possibly because of the problems caused by Hilary's absence – there was some talk of changing the format of the show. I never knew the details, but I think the plan was to have something like eight dragons. Only four or five would appear in each episode and we would all keep swapping places. I don't think Theo liked the idea of anyone else sitting in his seat, and he wasn't completely happy when production moved from London to Salford, so he decided to leave the panel. As did Hilary.

I've been writing this book while filming the 11th series with two new dragons: Kelly Hoppen and Piers Linney. It's always exciting to hear how new dragons assess business opportunities and Kelly and Piers bring something really fresh to the show, but there will undoubtedly be some people who think the Den isn't the same without Theo. Perhaps others will say it is better. It certainly feels very different.

I'd known Kelly socially before she joined the show so I knew we would get on. She's an interior designer and is fanatical and knowledgeable about every aspect of design. The papers tried to stir up trouble and question whether she was rich enough to be a dragon; all I can say is they obviously hadn't visited her house.

I had never heard of Piers before, but then he has made his fortune in a completely different field – cloud computing (whatever that is). He's much younger than the rest of the panel and I was really intrigued to see what he would bring to the programme. Very early on, a technology opportunity was pitched to us and I have got used to letting Peter take the lead on the questioning for those sorts of companies. When Piers had to tell Peter he was wrong about something, he was fully prepared to argue his point of view and left us in no doubt that he would be making his presence felt in the Den.

Another advantage of having Kelly on the panel is that she is incredibly knowledgeable about nutrition. The producers told us that in order to get more filming done they were shortening our lunch break, which meant eating in the green room. The problem with that – apart from the fact that I no longer had time to do a workout in my lunch break – was that the food in the green room wasn't exactly healthy. Having noticed that Kelly was getting her meals delivered from our hotel, I asked her to order meals for me too. So, instead of filling up on snacks and sandwiches, I got lean chicken and steamed veg, and I actually lost weight during the filming of the last series.

It also helps that Kelly's daughter Natasha has her own business – Honestly Healthy – that delivers nutritionally balanced (and delicious) snacks and meals direct to customers: the fridge in the green room is now packed with raw juices and seedy snacks, which is just the kind of food that keeps you going on a long day in the Den.

Although making *Dragons' Den* is almost always good fun, it can also be hard work. I get up at 7.30am for a session in the hotel's gym with a personal trainer. Then I'm in the car at 9am to head for the studio, followed by hair, make-up and breakfast, to be ready for filming at 10am. We used to get two days to film an episode, but budget cutbacks on series 11 mean we have 17 days to record 12 episodes. Inevitably that means working longer days, so we're usually on set until 8pm, or 8.30pm. By the time Peter opens the wine menu we are very ready for a drink.

I think my fighting with Peter in the early series made for good television, and we tried to get that going again during filming recently but we just can't falsify it. I've honestly never enjoyed making the programme more – we're just having lots of laughs. That doesn't mean there isn't the odd verbal punch-up, but we told Piers and Kelly when they started what we had all agreed between us a few years ago: what happens on set stays on set. On one of Piers's first days of filming, he and I fell out over something – I really can't remember what now – but as soon as filming finished, I stood up and went over and gave him a hug. 'Look we've had our first fall-out!' I said. We both laughed it off and by the time the five of us reached the restaurant that night I don't think either of us could recall what it had been about.

The viewing figures for series ten were much lower than for previous series – around 2 million an episode, down from 3.5 million – because they scheduled us against *I'm a Celebrity* and *Downton Abbey* on a Sunday night. Lower viewing figures meant fewer mentions in the media and I don't think we got a single 'pick of the day' review in the mainstream papers. I suppose I want to see that the BBC is still committed to the Den. They have brought in new producers who come from entertainment (rather than factual) backgrounds and it will be interesting to see if viewers notice a shift in emphasis when the show airs.

I know that the BBC has paid the licence for the show format to Sony (it's based on an original programme from Japanese TV) for another two years, which means there will be a 13th series. I honestly don't know if I'll be part of the panel then. I have mixed feelings about how much longer I should do it. There's a natural time to leave most situations, and I think it will soon be the right time for me to go.

Of course, it's completely possible that the BBC might not ask me back.

TWELVE

My Investments

In the first ten series of *Dragons' Den* I made 29 offers of investment, slightly more than half of which were joint investments with another dragon. Sadly, probably only around a half of those actually made it through the due diligence process. There was a time when the show attracted some bad headlines that said it was somehow offering fake investments and giving false hope to entrepreneurs, but the fact is that when we start to negotiate the details of a deal, things don't always turn out to be the way they were described in front of the cameras. Let me reassure any doubters: the Den is completely real, and it is my real money that I am investing, so you'll understand that I want to be sure the opportunity is just as it's described when it's pitched to us.

The due diligence process starts immediately after the recording of the show. The producers send me a DVD of the pitch, and my legal team watch it very closely. They then send an initial letter to the company I want to invest in, setting out everything we agreed in the studio: the amount, the percentage, whether or not the investment is in a parent company or just in the product in question and so on. If the investment was based on a patent, or confirmation of an order, my team will ask to see all the relevant paperwork.

They will also ask the entrepreneur a series of standard questions about the existing ownership of the company, the types of shares being issued and whether or not they have ever been bankrupt. Then they draw up contracts of employment for the entrepreneurs, and put in place structures to prevent them from taking dividends or hiking their salaries without the approval of the new chairman – me. Once my lawyer is happy, new shares are issued to me and I transfer the money.

Unlike other investment situations where you are sent a business plan before you meet the founders, in the Den we make our offers based on what is presented to us on the day. Even though we might spend an hour or more asking questions, there are always some details that don't come to light, which is why due diligence is so important. Usually these details aren't serious, but sometimes we find very good reasons why the investment can't go ahead – over the years we've come across unexpected holding companies, flawed accounts and faked orders.

There was one company, Kiddimoto, that Hilary and I wanted to invest in. We really liked the guy pitching to us, Simon Booth, and we really liked his products – wooden balance bikes for kids. We both wanted to take his business to the next level, but during due diligence we decided that we couldn't. The shareholder agreements for the company revealed that there was a secret shareholder. The company had actually been started by two people, and (as is fairly standard) they had given themselves one share each. But when one of them had left the company, the other carried on, put his own money in and issued himself with more shares. I can't remember how much he paid for those shares, but let's just say it was £500.

We asked Simon for the minutes of the meeting where the new shares had been issued, or the letter from the other shareholder confirming he didn't want to take part in the share issue. No such paperwork existed, which meant that his former partner could ask to be issued with the same number of shares for £500 *at any time*. Even if Simon turned Kiddimoto into a £100 million company, his ex-partner would always be entitled to buy half of it for £500!

'But he wouldn't do that,' said Simon when we told him.

'So ask him to sell his share to you.'

Simon asked him but he refused – he said he quite liked having a share in the company for sentimental reasons. There wasn't the option of starting a new company as the existing one was the owner of the patent. So Hilary and I had no choice but to pull out because at any point our holding in the company could be halved and there wouldn't be anything we could do about it. It hasn't stopped Simon making a success of the company – Kiddimoto is doing really well – but it would worry me if someone had that kind of power over my business.

As time has gone on, more and more investments the dragons try to make are failing to get through due diligence, and not because of a mistake or misrepresentation. I believe a big percentage of Den entrants now have no desire to get investment – they just want the publicity. As the only way you can guarantee your business will make the final edit is if you accept an offer, every single one of us has been in the situation where we've shaken hands in the studio, but as soon as the episode has been transmitted, the entrepreneurs involved coincidentally change their minds.

There is no doubt that appearing on *Dragons' Den* is good for business. I remember one of the early entrants was an inventor called Danny Bamping who made puzzles. I think we all made him an offer but he chose Theo and Rachel to be his investors. There was no great hurry to do the due diligence back then, so by the time the episode aired, the deal hadn't gone through. After transmission Danny secured so many orders that he no longer needed the investment. It was a wake-up call to all the dragons – if you don't get the due diligence done and dusted before transmission, you massively increase the chances that the deal won't go through.

In recent series, it has become something of a pattern. Hilary and I made an offer to invest in a company that makes dipping sauces, called Sweet Mandarin. The twins who developed the recipes and started the business kept delaying the due diligence and as soon as their episode aired, they wrote to us to say that they had had a rethink about bringing in outside investments because it was a family business. It might have been a coincidence, but a similar thing happened when Peter and I offered to invest in a frozen cocktail company called Rocktails. They came back to us and said that they had talked it over with their minority investor, who had said that he didn't want to dilute his holding so had made them a better offer.

With every series we get the feeling that more and more entrepreneurs may be there primarily to get publicity. In series ten, none of my offers were converted into investments, and I think the same thing happened to Hilary. It's difficult not to draw conclusions when their letter backing out of the deal arrives just after they've appeared on television, but unless we offer to invest in the first place, we can't know if they are genuine or not.

On the financial side, what I look for in the Den hasn't changed since the first series. I've always said I want a 20% return as a minimum, that means if I invest £100,000 in a business it should give me an income of £20,000 a year. After five years I'll have got my investment back, and anything after that is pure profit. What has changed, though, is what I look for in the entrepreneurs I back. Too many people come into the Den thinking that a dragon will sort everything out for them, so I try to assess how much of my time they will take up. I really want to see their hunger and their determination, and I instinctively pull back from anyone who thinks a dragon is a knight on a white charger who's going to make everything all right.

As I now have quite a few investments, I suppose I'm also becoming slightly fussier about the businesses I'll put money into. I want it to be a business I'll get excited about, not just one that makes a profit. I'm also looking for businesses that are a good fit with my existing portfolio, whether that's the health clubs, hotels, spas, or one of my other Den investments.

I think my style in the Den may have changed a bit too. In the past I was more eager to jump in and give my assessment, worried that another dragon would say what I wanted to say. But I've now realised that I can always add something and so I tend to hang back a bit more. In fact, one of the most fascinating things about the Den is hearing what the other dragons have to say: sometimes we are faced with bizarre or niche businesses, and yet we all find pertinent questions to ask. I've noticed that different dragons focus on different things: one might be concerned with return on capital, while another might ask about margins or marketing. It's very rare for there to be long silences in the Den, and we've all got our favourite questions for getting the relevant information out of people – even when we don't understand how their business makes money. 'So tell me how you got into this?' or 'Tell us something about yourself?' or 'What's the international potential for this product?'.

The maximum I have ever offered was £200,000, for a stake in the Wand Company, which made a TV remote control in the shape of a magic wand. Unfortunately, that was one of the occasions where the entrepreneurs decided against taking investment after transmission. However, I did get two £100,000 investments past due diligence: they were in Igloo, a refrigerated transport company, and another company that cleaned offices and commercial premises. In total I've probably invested a little under £1 million through the Den.

The traditional model for venture-capital investment has always been that out of ten investments you'll lose your money on seven, break even on two but with the tenth you'll make a fortune that dwarfs your losses on all the other investments. With angel investing, which is what we do in the Den, the participation of the angel (or dragon) skews those percentages quite a bit. I would say I've only lost money on about four in ten of my investments, but as two of my losses were both for £100,000, I think I'm only just breaking even. That said, if some of my current investments were sold, I think I'd end up with a very nice profit.

Without a doubt, my most lucrative investment has been in the electrical components company called Electro Expo that I talked about earlier. It had been run successfully for over a decade by Peter Moule before he came into the Den. Peter's pitch was one of the most memorable of all the series, for two reasons: firstly because he wore his glasses perched on his forehead (I've since asked him why he does this and he says it's his brand!) and secondly because he was already making £300,000 a year in profit but was asking us for £150,000 of investment. Clearly, he didn't really need our money.

Peter had invented something he called ChocBox, which is a little plastic box that makes connecting electrical cables together easier and safer. He was already selling a million units a year, but given that almost every electrician will need to join cables on every single job, he thought there was the potential to sell many more, and he recognised that he needed a dragon to get his business to the next level.

James and I invested together and we were able to make introductions that saw ChocBoxes stocked in far more retailers. Soon afterwards Peter's sales and profits took off. It became very clear that Peter really knew the DIY and components market, so James and I became drawn to investing in businesses that would work well alongside

Electro Expo. In fact, we could use our dividends from Electro Expo to invest in further businesses such as Blinds in a Box, Magnamole and Rapstrap which would effectively become subsidiaries of Electro Expo. It meant the new businesses would benefit not just from having me and James on board, but from Peter Moule's sector expertise as well. In a way, Peter became a sixth dragon.

However, as I've already said, tensions between me and James were building. It got to the stage where he avoided being in the same room as me, and he wouldn't shake my hand, so he wasn't getting involved in any of the board meetings. After James had left the Den, Peter Moule and I started to wonder why – given the success of Electro Expo – it had never been featured in any of the follow-up programmes. We thought it was unlikely the producers would ever feature the company now that James had left the show, and this led to a discussion about buying James out of the business. Peter had always had enough money to buy James's shares back, so he and James came to an arrangement. Peter now owns the vast majority of the business and I have 34%.

There are a number of ways I could realise my investment in Electro Expo – it could one day be sold to a bigger firm in the sector, and there might even be an option of listing the company. But for the time being I am happy to keep taking the dividends as the company grows. Whatever happens in the future, I have no doubt that Electro Expo has been the Den's greatest success story. Reggae Reggae Sauce, which Richard Farleigh and Peter Jones invested in, might have a higher profile but I'm pretty sure Electro Expo has bigger profits.

Another of my Den successes was investing in the stage-school company Razzamataz, which is run by Denise Hutton-Gosney. Denise gave us a great pitch but none of the other dragons could see the potential. I, however, had invested in their biggest rival – Stagecoach – several years before and had made a very nice return when it floated on the Stock Exchange. I thought I might be able to do the same with Razzamataz.

Since my investment, Denise has grown the business very successfully and it has actually done really well during the downturn. Razzamataz is a franchise model, and with lots of people getting made redundant in the past few years, low-cost franchises like Razzamataz have become really popular. Denise has also secured a contract from Thomson Holidays to run the stage schools in their resorts (a contract previously held by Stagecoach, which makes the deal that bit sweeter). We have no plans to sell at the moment, but I can see a company like Stagecoach making an offer at some point in the future. Until then, I am happy to hold on to my stake.

I still have an investment – alongside Peter Jones – in Worthenshaws, which makes a dairy-free alternative to ice cream. The company has been rebranded as Kirsty's, after the founder Kirsty Henshaw, and it has branched out into making 'free from' ready meals for people who have food allergies. There has been talk about a management buyout, and I hope to make a very nice return on my investment if and when that happens.

Of course, not all investments work out. Igloo Thermo Logistics lost £100,000 of my money because they got their accounting wrong and went into liquidation. The two founders then bought the company from the liquidators for a substantial discount, which was very nice for them, but a bit galling for Richard Farleigh and me who got nothing.

I lost another £100,000 in a cleaning company, which came as a complete shock. When the founder and one of his employees came into the Den I was really impressed with them. I saw real potential in both them and in their business, but they too went bust because they made one very stupid mistake. They put in a bid to clean the windows of a chain of nursing homes and based their bid on each home having an average of 50 rooms. It was only when they turned up on site that they realised most of the homes in the chain were much larger – some had 200 rooms – but they had a contract, and they had to fulfil it. That meant they were losing £50,000 a year, which left them with no option but to wind the company up.

I came close to having a third investment go into administration, but Glasgow Coffee Company Ltd, a coffee-shop franchise, went into liquidation before I got a chance to invest. When I did a bit of investigating, I found out that the owner, Umer Ashraf, had put a few companies into liquidation, which is something you have to do when you don't have the money to pay your tax and VAT. It offers you protection from creditors, but it doesn't stop you – as in the case of Glasgow Coffee Company Ltd – getting your landlord to transfer the lease into the name of the new company and continuing to operate on the same premises. Umer still wanted me to invest in the new company, but he couldn't answer my lawyer's questions adequately so I never put the money in.

I also lost money on an investment I made with Deborah in ProWaste, a company that recycled construction waste. After a while, Deborah and I started to get frustrated because we could never get the information we wanted from the founders. Whenever we asked for updates, they always seemed to stall and eventually we called a meeting with them where they offered to buy back our shares. The only problem was that they didn't have enough money to pay us the full amount, but by that stage Deborah and I were so fed up with them that we were just happy to recoup some of our investment and sold them back at a loss.

Normally, I try to invest in companies where I can add a lot of value, but in series nine I accidentally ended up with a stake in a record company, and I think it's fair to say I know as much about the music industry as I do about quantum physics. The truth is, I didn't mean to buy a stake in a record company at all, but one of the rules of the Den is that if you make an offer, you can't withdraw it unless the investment fails due diligence.

Ryan Ashmore and Liam Webb were 18 when they came into the Den with RKA Records. They were very enthusiastic and clearly loved their music, but what really got the dragons' attention was when they said that they only paid the acts they had signed to their label a 20% royalty and they kept 80%. We all thought that seemed a bit harsh, so I decided to make them an offer.

'I'm going to offer you a better deal than you give your artists,' I said. 'I'm going to offer you all the money, but I want 79% of your business.'

I was amazed when they said yes. I had made the offer to

highlight how unfair their contracts were, but they hadn't realised I was only trying to do them a favour by teaching them a lesson. In fact, it ended up being a lesson for me that cost me £50,000.

To be fair to them, the chance to work with a dragon on your first business is a great opportunity and they were probably right to accept my offer. Their eagerness meant that the due diligence was pretty painless and a few months later I found myself the majority shareholder in a record company.

What many people don't realise about investment is that it is usually accompanied by a contract of employment; after all, if you're putting your money into someone's business, you want the reassurance that they can't just walk away and that their behaviour will always reflect well on the business. Unfortunately, within about six months of the investment, Ryan and Liam left the company. Fortunately, they had already put me in touch with a guy called Kevin Savage who has a lot of experience in the music industry. So I called him up and asked him if he fancied having a stake in the business.

'Listen,' I said, 'I could buy the remaining shares for a tenner, but I can't run a record label. You can, so why don't you buy them for a tenner?'

I also realised that having a 21% stake wasn't big enough to incentivise him, so we agreed on a 49/51 split and renamed the business Bannatyne Music. And since Kevin came on board, the company has been doing really well. We've signed a boy band, Reconnected, who had been on *Britain's Got Talent*, and their first single got airplay on Radio 1 and entered the charts at number 32. I'm learning just how competitive the music industry is and how difficult it is to break an act if you're not Simon Cowell, but the Reconnected lads are great, and Kevin is very committed, so I'm really hopeful I'll get a return on my £50,000 investment.

Since the financial crisis, the atmosphere in the Den has started to change and the kinds of businesses coming to the dragons for investment are changing. Gone are the days when 'borrow £25,000 for any reason' flyers came through the door every day: entrepreneurs who would previously have got a business loan or taken equity out of their houses have found that those options are no longer open to them. On more than one occasion I've wondered how differently my career might have turned out if I hadn't been able to borrow money in the early days of Quality Care Homes.

The producers have changed the rules slightly to reflect this new reality. It used to be that the minimum you could ask for in the Den was £50,000, but they've dropped it to £30,000. It's the sort of money that prior to 2007 many people could have raised through personal loans and credit cards. Anyone with a mortgage could have probably extended their home loan by that amount with just a phone call to their bank.

More and more, when we ask entrepreneurs why they haven't put their own money in, they explain convincingly that they just couldn't borrow a penny. I can see it must be a hard choice for these entrepreneurs to take on an investor, because a few years ago they wouldn't have had to give up any equity to get their businesses off the ground. Even so, we dragons still prefer the person in front of us to have put their own money into a venture. Sweat equity is pretty hard to walk away from, but it's only when an entrepreneur stands to lose hard cash that they will fight tooth and nail for their business.

THIRTEEN

The Trouble with the Den

Another thing that's different in the Den these days is that we are seeing far more stupid inventions than in previous years. This might be because the producers know that idiotic gadgets make good television, but I do sometimes worry that *Dragons' Den* has done the United Kingdom a great disservice. We seem to have convinced people that what they need to become very successful is a unique and innovative product, even though such gadgets very rarely get backing from a dragon.

I have lost count of the ridiculous 'inventions' that have been brought into the Den. There was one for keeping the end of a cut cucumber fresh; someone tried to convince us cardboard beach furniture had a future; and I think we all burst out laughing when we were presented with the opportunity to put our money into false nails for cats! My own personal favourite is the man who brought us a single glove because he thought he could convince British motorists to wear it when they were driving abroad to remind them which side of the road they should be on!

While it's often obvious that a product is doomed to failure, we don't always get it right in the Den. The invention I personally regret not seeing the potential in is the Tangle Teezer hairbrush. I think we were all swayed by a comment Deborah made – that the design was too similar to a brush she used on her horses – and that made us think the Tangle Teezer patent wouldn't stand up. It was also a difficult presentation because the founder, a really nice guy called Shaun Pulfrey, seemed not to be listening and was shouting at us. In fact this was because he's a little hard of hearing. He left without an investor but almost immediately after his episode aired, he secured a supply deal with Boots and his business has never looked back. I made the follow-up show about Tangle Teezer, and it was only then that I realised how easy Shaun would have been to work with. I asked him if he still needed investment, but he said he would only give half as much equity away at that stage. And of course now he doesn't need any investment at all. For me, Tangle Teezer is the one that got away.

I think part of the problem with the gadget-makers who come to the Den is that they think they have already done the hard work. A lot of them assume that since they've come up with an idea and had a prototype made, all they need to do is add a little dragon magic and they can retire to the Caribbean and wait for their cheques to arrive. The gadget entrepreneurs tend to have the feel of a lottery-ticket holder about them: they think they're going to get really rich, really quickly. I don't know what the odds of making millions off a new gadget are, but I bet they're closer to the lottery's odds of 14 million to one than the odds-on sure thing some Den entrants seem to think they are.

Obviously, a lot of people who come up with an invention truly believe that their gadget will improve the world, but even if their idea is a good one, there's still a very strong chance it will make for a bad business. If you've watched the Den you'll have seen us pull apart one patent application after another. Despite ten series of this, novice entrepreneurs still think a patent will protect them. I can only assume they've been in the kitchen putting the kettle on every time it's happened. We've seen people who have spent tens of thousands of pounds on patents and trademarks that just don't add any value to a business at all – but they add a tidy sum to the balance sheets of patent attorneys.

The people who get into the most trouble with patents are those who think they are protecting their idea. Patents can't – and don't – protect ideas, they can only protect new technologies and innovative processes. It's not enough to say that you've got an idea for a cyclonic vacuum cleaner, you need to have a working prototype using demonstrably new technology (and, by the way, it took James Dyson over 5,000 attempts to get the right prototype for his cyclone cleaner).

Also, just because you've never heard of a gadget like yours before, it doesn't mean someone, somewhere hasn't had the same idea and already patented it. One of the benefits of trying to obtain a patent is that you will at least find out if your product infringes someone else's patent.

Even if you are awarded a patent, it still can't prevent rival products being developed. When I look at the treadmills in my health clubs, they all have a list of their patents on them, but none of those have stopped other manufacturers producing their own treadmills. In series 11, we had a lovely guy come into the Den to pitch a business built around a new type of reed for use in woodwind instruments that was easier to attach. He had applied for a patent, but even if it was eventually granted, it won't prevent another reed manufacturer thinking 'Oh, easily attachable reeds are a good idea, let's see if there's another way of attaching them.' I could see a couple of ways of redesigning them and I had never held a woodwind instrument before! What the entrepreneur had failed to acknowledge was that the people who buy reeds won't care which method is used for attaching the reeds, only that they attach easily. He might have had a good idea, but it wasn't a *defendable* patent.

Patents take years to be granted and the process of applying for them can be a distraction for an entrepreneur. It can give them a false sense of security, and it can drain their business of money that would be better spent on marketing, recruitment or even paper clips.

My other concern about entrepreneurs who rely on patents to make their business case for them is that there is no such thing as the Patent Police. Even if you have a great invention, even if you are granted a brilliant patent, there is nothing to stop someone copying your idea and your methodology and getting your product to market. It will be down to you to enforce your patent, and that will cost you yet more money. Imagine that the company you need to sue is making more money from the gadget in question than you are: will the money you require to enforce your patent be available to you? Now imagine that the company infringing your patent is Apple, or Unilever, or Boeing, the kind of company with a legal department so big that they can allocate someone to respond to your lawyer's letters up to the point where you can no longer afford for your lawyer to continue. Or imagine that a factory in the suburb of some industrial city in China you've never heard of starts infringing your patent. Even if you went over there all guns blazing with a team of lawyers, you'd probably find the factory would have mysteriously stopped operations the day before you got there and moved on somewhere else. And as there's no governing body that will award you compensation for your losses, you might want to consider if the money you spend on patents would be better spent on marketing or improving your product.

The really surprising thing about the innovations and patents we see is that the people who come to pitch to us don't seem to have realised that none – not one – of the dragons has built a business based on a patent. None of us has even done anything particularly unique. Simon Woodroffe didn't invent sushi, I wasn't the first person to put single bedrooms in nursing homes and Peter Jones wasn't the first guy to sell mobile-phone components (if that is what he does – I'm still not quite sure). All we did was take an existing industry or product and do it better than our competitors.

Far too much emphasis is put on innovation. Newspapers and financial magazines are always looking to write about overnight successes because they're a better story than the diligent plodders. Similarly, they want to recommend shares that will give spectacular returns over the short term, rather than modest growth over the long term.

None of the dragons got rich overnight. None of us had a lucky break. None of us, I think I'm right in saying, became millionaires from our first business. We all muddled through, made mistakes, learnt from them, then started doing things smarter and faster. It's no surprise that my two biggest investments in the Den were in a refrigerated freight business and a cleaning business: you don't need to innovate to get our attention. Or our money.

Of course, it's not just wasting time and money on patents that Den entrants get wrong. We're still seeing people order thousands of items of stock before they've secured a single customer, only to have to store those goods at considerable cost (and then have their stock decrease in value as it becomes less fashionable/topical/cutting-edge). We're still seeing people who value their businesses way too highly, and people who don't know the difference between profit and turnover.

I worry that the Den sometimes gives the impression that a good business also has to be a big business. Obviously, as investors, we are looking to put our money into ventures that have scale and opportunities to grow, but many people come into the Den with very good businesses, they just happen not to be *investable* businesses. Either they're too small, or they offer limited chances for growth, or they're too reliant on the founder to succeed. I don't like to think of viewers getting the impression that these might be bad businesses. Some of them are great businesses making great products and employing several people while making their owner a decent enough living along the way. Even if that's all a business does, that makes it a great business, and a great success story. It just might not be a great investment opportunity.

A good example of a decent business that wasn't a great investment was Trunki, the children's suitcase manufacturer. I've read several times that Trunki is one of the Den's most successful rejects, and I've heard that the founder, Rob Law, likes to say that his company is one of the investments that got away. But the truth is that it was never an investable proposition for a dragon.

When Rob came into the Den in 2006 he was offering us a non-negotiable 10% of his company for £100,000. If we leave aside that there was no way his company was worth £1 million at the time and that Theo easily broke his prototype, you only have to look at the last set of accounts Rob lodged with Companies House to see he wasn't offering us a decent investment opportunity. His accounts for the year ending 2011 show that shareholder funds in the company were roughly £1,360,000, which would mean a dragon's 10% stake would have been worth £136,000 – that's not much of a return over five years. But actually, when you look at the figures more closely, you see there's a premium on some of the shares that reduces the real value of the shareholder funds to around £1,113,000, taking the value of the 10% we were being offered to just over £111,000. That's just 11% over five years. Even with low interest rates, we'd have been better off putting our money in the bank where there was no risk to our capital. We were absolutely right not to invest, and I have no regrets over Trunki whatsoever.

But, by contrast, when I look a Tangle Teezer's figures, it's clear that we really did miss out on an opportunity. Shaun

Pulfrey was offering us 15% in exchange for £80,000. We never even got round to negotiating with Shaun, but it's probable we could have got him up to 20%. Tangle Teezer's latest accounts at Companies House show that 20% would now be worth £200,000, which is why I maintain it's the only investment we've let get away.

Another worry I have is that the *Dragons' Den* format makes business look too easy – I've always said it's *simple*, but it's rarely easy. Because pitches are edited down to a maximum of about ten minutes' screen time, we don't really get a chance to show just how hard some people have had to work to get into the Den. And as most episodes end with a congratulatory handshake, I wonder if some viewers see getting investment as the happy end of the story – in a way, *Dragons' Den* is a bit like those romantic comedies where the film ends with a wedding and we never get to see what a hard slog the marriage is. I don't know how else to explain that after ten series – and numerous books by most of the dragons – we're still seeing people coming in with a very shaky understanding of what being in business is really all about.

I've also had concerns about the focus the programme puts on the wealth of the dragons, the big valuations that companies put on themselves, or on projected revenue figures that are astronomical. It obviously makes for entertaining TV, but it's a shame if that focus leads us to underappreciate smaller businesses in this country, because it's those businesses that I think almost anyone is capable of starting and running successfully if they're prepared to work hard. It's those businesses that should be seen as inspirational –

and aspirational – rather than the headline-grabbing deals about teenagers selling apps for millions.

I'm frequently asked why so many businesses fail, and one of the reasons has to be that new entrepreneurs are often shocked by just how much hard work it takes to get a business off the ground. Too many people have the view that they will only have to put in the long hours for a few months – a few years at the most – but building a truly successful business can take a decade. That's a decade of no holidays, no weekends, missing important family events and putting the rest of your life on hold. Some people thrive on that stress, but many can't handle it. They just throw in the towel too soon.

Let me give you an example. One of my Den investments was failing to take off and the founder felt sure that the route to success lay in getting orders from American customers. As a shareholder, I had some say over how the company's finances were spent and to start with I said I wouldn't approve the travel expenses involved if she couldn't get more sales in the UK. Eventually, after several months, I relented and she went off to the States. While she was there I got lots of positive texts about how many orders had been placed. It seemed I had been wrong, and that America was the land of plenty after all.

When she got home, I expected to receive a detailed report about who the new customers were and what levels of orders she had achieved. Instead all I got was a message to say that she had been flooded and all her orders had been turned to mush. Oh, yes, and the cat ate her homework too.

I can't be sure, but it felt to me that she might have

reached the point where she'd had enough and couldn't take the stress any more. Now I know Americans are known for talking up prospects and she wouldn't be the first person to have been taken in but it seemed to me that she just didn't have the stomach for continuing the fight. She gave up after that. I wouldn't have invested in her if I hadn't thought her product was a good one – it's still a product someone else could make a business out of, but they would have to be prepared to work harder and longer than she was prepared to do.

I've always said that being in business is simple – if you can buy something for 50p and sell it for £1 then you've got the basics – but I would never want anyone to think it's easy. It's not. It's bloody hard work. But it's also one of the most rewarding things you can do with your life. You should never let a bit of hard work put you off.

FOURTEEN

The Life of a Dragon

When I agreed to join *Dragons' Den*, I didn't realise that I would become a celebrity. I had taken part in TV programmes before, and had got quite used to strangers saying 'Don't I know you from somewhere?', but nothing can really prepare you for the recognition you get when you're part of a hit TV show. I remember that the very day after the first episode aired in 2005, I went into a coffee shop around the corner from my London flat and the man serving me said 'You're the 22% guy!'.

At first, people just knew me as a dragon, then after a series they knew my name, and by the end of series two they had even started to spell my name right (it's very rare these days that I get a letter addressed to 'Mr Ballantyne').

One of the first things that happened after the Den became successful was that the price people were willing to pay me for public speaking skyrocketed. It had previously been somewhere around the £5,000 mark – which isn't bad for a few hours' work – but with the name recognition TV gave me, that quickly reached £20,000 and at one point was £25,000 (it's slipped back down to £20,000 now that everyone is trying to cut costs). Then I was asked to write a book, then another – I'm a little surprised to realise that this is now my seventh.

I was also asked to make lots of different TV programmes, from business makeover shows like *Mind Your Own Business* and *Seaside Rescue* to game shows like *All Star Family Fortunes* and *Who Wants to Be a Millionaire*. I've also been a guest judge on *Britain's Got More Talent* and I've appeared on the stage at the Royal Albert Hall as part of a gala performance of Captain Beaky in aid of UNICEF. These things are always great fun to do.

On a couple of occasions I've been asked to do *Celebrity Big Brother* and *I'm a Celebrity . . . Get Me Out of Here*, and in 2013 I was approached to appear in *Splash!*, the diving show hosted by Tom Daley, but I'd rather watch all of those than be in them. There's a part of me that would actually be quite interested in going into the jungle, just to prove I could survive, but I think you risk ending up in a bracket of people seen as just wanting fame for fame's sake. If they would just leave a bunch of celebrities alone in the jungle with a couple of cameras for a few weeks to see if we could do a Bear Grylls, then I might be a bit more interested.

Some of the other TV programmes I've done have been for Comic or Sport Relief or Children in Need. Apart from lending support to causes I believe in – I have been on the board of Sport Relief for a number of years – they usually involve learning a new skill. I took part in a show called *Only*

Fools on Horses for Sport Relief where a bunch of celebrities were taught to showjump. It was a lot of fun – until I was thrown from my horse and broke my arm fairly early on in the recording. A couple of years later, I found out I had actually been far more seriously injured. Long after my arm had healed, I kept having trouble with my back and eventually went to see a doctor about it. An X-ray revealed I had cracked three vertebrae, and the most likely cause was my fall from the horse.

A couple of years after that, the dragons were asked to take part in *Let's Dance for Comic Relief* and Deborah, Peter and I learned a bit of ballroom. We didn't win, but at least I didn't break anything.

In 2012, my agent got a call asking if I would take part in the *Great British Bake-Off* for Comic Relief. As I had time in my diary I said yes, but I didn't really give it too much thought until a couple of days before filming when I realised I had never baked in my life! The point of the show was to encourage people to make cakes to sell to raise money for Comic Relief, so I realised that I had better learn to bake, otherwise I wouldn't be helping the cause very much.

I went to see the chef at Charlton House and he came up with some recipes for me – including some very fiddly biscuits shaped like ice-cream cones – and although I didn't win the competition, I did discover (to everyone's surprise) that I am not a bad baker. A few weeks after the show aired, the estate where I live in the north-east, Wynyard Park, was organising its own charity event and they decided to have a cake sale. They asked me to contribute one, but the timings didn't work out. However, I suggested that they raffle a cake of mine and when I got home I'd bake it and deliver it to the highest bidder. So I can now claim that someone has paid probably far more for a cake made by me – £1,875, to be precise – than anyone has ever paid for cakes made by Jamie Oliver and Nigella Lawson put together. I can't quite believe I'm saying this, but I really do enjoy baking.

One of the most interesting TV programmes I've been involved with in the past few years was a documentary for CBBC about a condition called 'face blindness' which causes difficulty in recognising people, in some cases even if the sufferer knows them very well. I didn't realise until fairly recently – after reading about it in a newspaper – that it's something I've suffered from all my life. Thankfully I am not too badly affected by it, but I met a couple of girls during filming who cannot recognise their friends at school or their own parents. It is incredibly difficult for them and they are having to learn different coping strategies. I hope that since meeting me, even though my own problem is nowhere near as severe, they have realised it is possible to have face blindness and still have a successful career.

After my own diagnosis, I look back at certain incidents in my life from a different perspective. I remember in the early days of Bannatyne Fitness, when we were still running the company out of a Portakabin, a guy came in to do some photocopying. I could tell he recognised me so I pretended I knew who he was, but after a few minutes of small talk, he slammed down the lid of the photocopier: I had clearly pissed him off somehow.

'You don't know who I am, do you?' he said.

I had to admit that I didn't.

'We met two days ago. You interviewed me for the manager's job. You gave me the job.'

I couldn't explain to him why I didn't recognise him, but I didn't. Now that I have an explanation for it – the proper name for the condition is prosopagnosia – I find it easier to deal with, though it still causes problems: being well-known actually makes it harder because people tend to remember meeting me. But I have learnt to cope with it, and I get a lot of help from my PA, Kim, who always writes down the names of everyone who comes in to meet me. The problem is that I can have a meeting with someone in the afternoon, then see them again in the evening and I genuinely won't know who they are. People may just think I'm rude, but I really don't mean to be, and it was great to be able to make a TV programme that explained the condition.

We knew that *Dragons' Den* had been promoted into a different league when we first started being parodied. It's a very strange experience watching TV and suddenly seeing someone do an impression of you. I thought the *Harry & Paul* spoof was a bit wicked, especially to Deborah, but it was also very funny. Harry Enfield actually trains at the same gym as me in London so I see him there occasionally. He was telling me one time how they were planning to do Hilary when she joined the show – he didn't tell me they were going to do her as the Dead Dragon!

There are very few downsides to being a celebrity, as far as I can see. The people who approach you in the street are almost always kind and say nice things, and when your agent calls you never know what new opportunity has just cropped up. I also get invited to join clubs that would never normally have a scruffy kid from Clydebank in their ranks, and find myself sitting next to amazing people at charity events. Whether that's another famous person or an aid worker or an injured army officer, one of the best things I get to do is meet a remarkable range of people. However, there is one invitation that still stands out: in 2010, I received a letter from Buckingham Palace inviting me to have dinner with the Queen.

Nobody ever knows why they're invited by the Queen, but I understand this is something she has always done as a way of staying informed. Every so often, a group of people who – I presume – have done something noteworthy or worthwhile (like senior people in public life and chief executives of businesses and charities) get invited to the Palace. On the night Joanne and I went, the other guests included the Director General of the BBC and Bear Grylls and his wife.

We were taken into one of the beautiful reception rooms, and we all introduced ourselves and then looked at the art and artefacts in the room, which are all, of course, extremely valuable. It was a bit like being in a very exclusive museum. Then it was announced that Her Majesty would be joining us and the Queen and Prince Philip came and shook everybody's hand.

Then there was a bell telling us to go to sit down as dinner was served. The next three hours were among the most surreal of my life. I just kept thinking 'What's a toerag from Clydebank doing having dinner here?' When the Queen decided to leave – it was probably meticulously timed – she and Prince Philip simply thanked everyone for coming and then wandered off up to the private rooms. Shortly afterwards, the rest of us got back into our cars and left. It's the sort of event that, as soon as it's over, you can't quite believe was actually real.

It would have been pretty easy over the past decade to have let the media opportunities that have come my way distract me from the thing that gave me a public profile in the first place – being successful in business. But given the way the economy has been, there was never a chance of that happening . . .

FIFTEEN

Thanks, Gordon

Since 2007, we've seen some of the toughest trading conditions anyone in business can remember. In my opinion, Gordon Brown was a great chancellor, but when Tony Blair resigned and he moved next door to Number 10 Downing Street, things instantly started to go downhill.

Brown became Prime Minister in June 2007. Barely a month later, in July, two hedge funds run by Bear Stearns had to close because they had lost almost all their clients' money. In August the financial markets became paralysed by fears about subprime lending in America, and in September queues started forming outside Northern Rock because it had technically gone bust. Brown – who had promised to end 'boom and bust' economics – and his chancellor Alistair Darling seemed to be taken as much by surprise at these events as the rest of us.

Obviously it's a coincidence that Brown's leaving Number 11 came at the same time as the start of the credit crunch, but the politicians made such a balls-up of getting us through the crisis that they have to take some of the blame for the mess we're still in now. First they dropped VAT to 15%, then they put it back up to 17.5%. When the Coalition came in they hiked it to 20% – and then they applied it to pasties before withdrawing it from pasties! The changes in VAT alone indicate a lack of leadership. I know the international situation has been dire for the past six years, but politicians in the UK have failed to make things any better and that has had a massive impact on my business.

However, back in the summer of 2007, I watched the headlines and felt impervious to what was going on. The previous year we had signed our ten-year loan with Anglo Irish, and as long as we kept making our payments I didn't think I had any reason to worry. I had a contract to pay 1.65% above LIBOR that no one could take away from me. In 2016, when the loan period ended, I couldn't see that we'd have any problems getting additional lending, especially as by then we'd have paid off £90 million and have a better debt-to-asset ratio. The idea that the economic problems could drag on for a decade seemed utterly ridiculous. As I write this in 2013, that now seems highly likely. It feels like the 2016 deadline is racing towards us like a runaway train carrying several tons of bricks.

From 2007 to 2010, the alarming news stories kept coming, and I kept expecting to feel some pain for my business. Surely with all those bad headlines, with all those businesses collapsing, people would start tightening their belts and cancelling their gym memberships? After all, isn't that what's supposed to happen in a recession: people cancel the non-essentials and focus on keeping a roof over their head and food on the table? Even when the FTSE 100 lost nearly half its value (in 2008 it had been over 6000 points, in March 2009 it was barely above 3500) things still seemed all right at Bannatyne Fitness. Not only were our membership numbers holding up, we were actually making more profit per member (largely due to the spas, as members were paying extra for treatments). Every month I pored over our figures expecting to see increased numbers of cancellations, but that just didn't happen. In fact, something really surprising happened: our profits went up.

When we had taken out our loan with Anglo Irish, the LIBOR rate was just above the Bank of England base rate of 4.75% (historically, it has usually been just a fraction higher than the base rate). For those of us that remember the 1990s, when rates reached 15%, this seemed incredibly low. Over the next year, rates started to creep up and by the summer of 2007, LIBOR was close to 6%. Although that doesn't sound like much of a rise, the impact of a 1% increase on a loan of £180 million isn't as trivial as it sounds. However, as long as the majority of our members didn't leave, our margins meant we had no trouble making the repayments. We were also insulated because we had taken out a 'cap and collar' on the loan.

Throughout my career I have been a big fan of fixing professional fees and limiting the impact of interest-rate changes, as businesses do best when they can plan their costs with certainty. When we took out the Anglo Irish loan, we also paid an extra fee for the 'cap and collar' deal: it meant that the rate they would charge us couldn't rise above the 'cap' at the top of the scale, or drop below the 'collar' at the bottom. The risk of this is that if interest rates plummet you may end up paying more than you need to, but the benefit is that you know you don't have to worry about interest rates skyrocketing as they did in the 1990s.

I've always treated these products like a form of insurance, and as we routinely pay for insurance, I have no problem paying the extra to have that peace of mind. Given that our loan was pegged to LIBOR – which we now know was easily manipulated by unscrupulous bankers – I'm an even bigger fan of deals that offer security.

The Bank of England base rate stayed above 5% for over a year and during that time the cap on our rate saved us money. Then in August 2008, as the financial crisis deepened, the Bank of England began to cut the base rate rapidly to relieve the pressure on mortgage payers and business owners. Thanks to the cap and collar, we started to benefit from lower repayments and by the end of the year, the base rate was just 2%, with LIBOR fractionally higher. A 3% reduction on a loan of £180 million provided us with a very welcome windfall, and it was money that went straight onto our bottom line. It also allowed us to put over £1 million into our charitable trust. When things felt like they should have been getting tougher, Bannatyne Fitness was actually in great shape.

Then, in March 2009, the Bank of England slashed its rate to 0.5% and LIBOR followed suit. It was a sign of just how badly the wider economy needed government support, but it provided a welcome boost for business. It's a very odd feeling when you're standing in the middle of a storm but not getting wet. It was as if the Bannatyne Group was standing under a low-interest-rate umbrella. But of course, whether we realised it or not, we were going to get soaked eventually.

The first thing that started to cause us trouble was inflation. Since 2007, inflation (based on the Consumer Prices Index) has almost always been above the government's target of 2%. On a couple of occasions it's been over 5%. I don't know what the average over the past six years has been, but I reckon it's somewhere around the 3.5% mark.

Normally, inflation doesn't have a big impact on our business because when costs go up, we are able to put our prices up. But when there's a recession going on, and when members might be looking at ways to cut back their monthly budgets, we didn't feel we were in a position to pass on our increased costs. That meant our margins were going to get squeezed. It was just a gentle pinch at first, but over the years it started to feel like being gripped in a vice. Let me give you a very simple illustration: let's just say you run a business that has annual costs of £100,000 and annual turnover of £120,000. A 3.5% increase in your costs takes them to £103,500 in the first year, and they rise to £107,122 in the second year. After six years of inflation at 3.5% you start to make a loss.

If you're not in a position to put your prices up, then all you can do is keep a very tight control on your costs, which is exactly what we have done. We've looked at all our contracts with suppliers and negotiated either a reduction or a rebate. Where possible, we've sourced cheaper suppliers, and we've made companies compete for our business: we've gone to Company X to say that Company Y has offered us a better deal and asked them to beat it. Inflation has still had an impact, but we have contained its effects as much as possible.

It was just as inflation was starting to sting that the new Coalition government announced a change that I knew instantly was going to hurt us very badly indeed. In George Osborne's first emergency budget the new chancellor announced that – as of January 2011 – VAT would be raised to 20%. I knew as I sat watching him on television that it would be a disaster for Bannatyne Fitness. At least with inflation, there are things you can do to lessen its impact by controlling your costs, but with VAT it's the government that has control.

Just about the only way you can respond to a VAT rise is to put your prices up. But as the economy slipped into a double-dip recession we didn't want to risk giving our members a reason to reconsider whether they could afford their membership fee. Our only option was to swallow the increase.

The impact of a VAT rise on a business like ours is far worse than creeping inflation because it applies to turnover not profit. In 2011 our turnover was roughly £120 million, which meant that the 2.5% VAT rise instantly reduced our profits by £3 million. If it hadn't been for the historically low interest rates, then we would really have been in trouble.

In many of my books on how to start and run businesses, I have written about the importance of performing what is known as a sensitivity analysis. It's something that not enough businesses do, but it was a tool that gave me a lot of comfort as we negotiated our way through 2010.

You carry out a sensitivity analysis by looking at each of your major costs, and each of your major income streams, and seeing what would happen if one of them went down – or up – by X%. By manipulating the figures in a spreadsheet, you can see how sensitive your business is to rises in costs, or falls in revenue. Some business owners are comfortable with a very narrow margin, but I had always sought to give my businesses a buffer of 40%. I had never really thought we'd ever need such a wide margin, but I was bloody glad I'd insisted on it as we watched our costs creep up and our income hold steady.

The next threat to the business proved to be the most serious yet, and it is the one I continue to struggle with as I write. It turned out that the deal that was keeping us in profit – that wonderful, magical, super-cheap Anglo Irish loan – was about to cause us an awful lot of pain.

Like RBS, Halifax and Lloyds in the UK, Anglo Irish required a massive government bailout. It had lent vast amounts of money to Irish homeowners, developers and buy-to-let investors, and when the Irish property bubble burst it was completely overexposed and the Irish government had to step in.

If that had been all that had happened, we wouldn't have been affected: after all, our contract was fixed for ten years. So long as we kept making the repayments, we had nothing to worry about. Or so I thought. However, the financial situation continued to worsen in Ireland and the country had to receive a bailout from the EU. Then, in 2009, Anglo Irish Bank had to be nationalised. Again, this didn't trouble me at first because I didn't see that it mattered who we owed the money to, so long as we kept paying it back.

The trouble really started for us when new banking regulations forced the banks to recapitalise. Banks were instructed to increase their capital levels – that is, the amount of money they held in relation to the amount they lent out – and this immediately led to the 'credit crunch', because instead of lending money out, they started to hoard it. In 2010, regulators decided that many banks were still posing a risk to the system, so they set even higher capital levels. This meant that banks didn't just reduce their lending, they actively started to try and foreclose on existing loans to get the capital out of the borrower's asset – either a business or a property – and back onto their own balance sheet. Any borrower who was in danger of breaching their covenants started to get nervous.

As part of the nationalisation, Anglo Irish Bank was renamed the Irish Bank Resolution Corporation. IBRC was effectively charged with calling in debts for the good of the nation. In 2010, we received a letter from them asking for a revaluation of the business. It was at this point that our umbrella developed a pretty big rip in the fabric.

SIXTEEN

Into Survival Mode

At this stage, it was really only the fact that the Bank of England base rate remained at 0.5% that allowed us to continue to operate with confidence. Throughout 2010, we knew that the VAT hike was coming and we knew any increase in the rate of interest we were paying would squeeze our margins so much that our profits after tax would be negligible. When a business stops making a profit, it hardly needs saying that it becomes extremely vulnerable and jobs are put at risk.

But while Bannatyne Fitness was desperate to keep paying the low 1.65% above LIBOR, our newly nationalised lender was equally keen for us to pay more. The fact that we were making our repayments and paying off £10 million of the principal each year wasn't enough for the bureaucrats who ran the bank; they were under an obligation to raise as much money for the Irish taxpayer as possible. Hence the request to revalue the business.

When Bannatyne Fitness had taken out the loan in 2006,

there were over 200 pages of conditions: it's always a good idea to read the small print. The first clause that now took on more significance than we could have imagined in 2006 was the rule that allowed the bank to revalue the business on every anniversary of the loan. This is standard – it's been a clause in most of the business loans I have ever taken out – but throughout my career it's been pretty meaningless: the value of my businesses have always gone up. All a revaluation would tell us was that we were worth more. At least that was the view from 2006. Rereading that clause in 2010 was a bit uncomfortable.

The reason it worried us was this: inflation was reducing our margins and VAT was about to take a massive bite out of profits. This meant our profits were in danger of falling below the level we had predicted at the time we took out the loan, which in turn meant we risked breaching one of our covenants.

We were also in danger of breaching the covenant on loan-to-value (LTV). As I've already said, businesses are valued as a multiple of profit and historically that multiple in the health-club industry had been ten. That meant the £3 million wiped off our profits by swallowing the VAT hike took a whopping £30 million off our valuation. But it was actually worse than that: since the start of the recession, multiples in most industries had been falling, and in our sector it had dropped to eight. A health-club business with profits of £20 million would now be valued at £160 million instead of £200 million.

We knew that if IBRC found us in breach the consequences could be disastrous: they would be within their rights to call in the loan. In the same situation, another lender would probably be happy to slap us with a monthly monitoring fee, put us on a higher interest rate and make more money from us that way, but IBRC had a mandate to recover money for the Irish taxpayer. They would rather have the full £120 million we still owed them at that point than an extra couple of hundred thousand a month in punitive charges.

In normal financial times, we would have looked to refinance and pay off the loan before they had a chance to call it in, but the credit crunch meant that wasn't an option. Effectively, calling in the loan would mean IBRC activating its charge over the company and putting it up for sale. And just as when a house gets repossessed, the lender doesn't care about getting the highest bid, all they want is enough to cover the outstanding loan: they would make sure they got their money, but I could be left with nothing.

This was a crazy situation – after all, Bannatyne Fitness was still making a profit, we were still paying down our debts – but it was also frighteningly real. It just seemed unbelievable that a business that was so healthy it was paying off £2.5 million of its debts every quarter could be put at risk on a technicality. Sometimes I would look at our newly built HQ, or visit one of our new spas, and it seemed impossible that such vibrant, exciting businesses could also be troubled businesses, but they were. Our only option was to make sure we did not breach those covenants. All of a sudden, the Bannatyne Group found itself in survival mode.

At the next board meeting, I discussed the situation with my senior team, particularly Nigel, my chief executive, and Chris Watson, my finance director. We did our own calculations on our valuation and agreed that we would be incredibly close to that 58% threshold. We just could not risk the bank undertaking a valuation at that time. We also calculated that – because we were paying off the capital amount by £2.5 million every three months – we would soon have paid back enough to put our LTV ratio back well below the limit. All we had to do was stall.

So the first thing I did was write to all the directors of the bank. Anyone can do this – you simply get their names and addresses from Companies House (it only takes a few minutes and a couple of quid if you do it online). It's something I've done a few times with companies I've been in dispute with. The trick is to send all correspondence by recorded delivery to arrive at the directors' houses on a Saturday morning; that way you maximise the chances that they will actually open the letter and read it!

In those letters I explained that the revaluation was a waste of money and therefore not in the interest of their shareholders. I also said it was causing a rift between my company and theirs. As expected, a few of them wrote back and, after taking a couple of weeks to consider my response – remember, I was trying to slow things down as much as possible – I replied to them and picked holes in some aspect of their argument. And so it went on for a few weeks. Then when the valuation team got in touch, we told them that they couldn't possibly carry out a valuation while we were in negotiations with the directors.

Although I was incredibly angry with the way we were being treated, I have to admit there was also a bit of me that enjoyed the fight. It had been a few decades since my back had been against the wall, and there's something very primal that happens when you find yourself in a battle to survive. Something about the process – while it was absolutely terrifying – was also a little electrifying. No matter what they threw at me, I was ready to throw everything I had back at them. It wasn't that different from when someone threatened one of my kids: there's something deep within me that is going to do whatever it takes to protect the people – and the businesses – I love.

We managed to delay the revaluation by nine months, by which time we had paid off another £7.5 million of the principal. Nevertheless, when we eventually received the revaluation report, the bank deemed that we were in breach by £2.5 million and they wanted to know what we proposed to do about it. I wrote back and told them that I wanted to enact my right to remedy.

I had read every clause of the 200-page contract myself and this is something I would recommend every entrepreneur does. I know it can be daunting if you're inexperienced, but you can always google the things you don't understand. If you leave the small print to your lawyer or your accountant, you won't know if they've missed something and, crucially, you won't have all the information you need to plan for the future. Because I had read the contract myself, I knew we had the right to remedy, and because I'd known about that right for a while, I had already worked out what the remedy would be.

I told the bank I was going to use the £3 million I had on deposit with them. Their reply, to paraphrase, was 'What the hell are you talking about?'. They were so disjointed, and so inept, that they did not realise I had a personal account with them in which I had £3 million – the £3 million I had saved from the hive-up and put away for a rainy day. I was actually just offering them money I wouldn't have had if they hadn't given us a payment holiday!

I told them to give me the details of the account they wanted the £2.5 million transferred into and said they could keep it as security until we had paid back another £2.5 million. 'But,' I added, 'I do not accept that we are in breach; I think you have made errors in your valuation and I reserve the right to sue you for loss of interest.'

Their response to my letter was to call a meeting with us. They suggested a date, but when we checked our diaries we found that Nigel couldn't make it. They suggested another date but, unfortunately, I was going to be unavailable on that day. We managed to string this along for about six weeks, and when we did finally sit down to discuss the technicalities of their valuation, they agreed to waive the breach – the risk of me suing them for loss of interest wasn't worth the hassle.

I can't tell you how relieved we all were. We had found ourselves in an incredibly tight spot, but we'd also found a way out of it. Chris and Nigel had been fantastic. However, just as our sense of achievement was dying down, we got a letter from the bank confirming that they'd waive the breach – but only on the condition we kept £2.5 million of that £3 million in their account.

I was so angry. That wasn't what we had agreed in the meeting, so I took another deep breath and patiently wrote back to them. I pointed out that they had come to our office, we had had a meeting in good faith, we had all shaken hands on the outcome, and now they were going back on their word. 'How can we trust you?' I asked.

It was quite a match of postal tennis, but eventually they backed down when they realised we were so close to having paid off the £2.5 million that there really wasn't any point in continuing.

We had survived. Until the next valuation, that is.

SEVENTEEN

Competition Makes You Stronger

The situation with Anglo Irish hasn't been the only threat to the business in recent years. The health-club sector has been shaken up by the arrival of low-cost gyms, although when they first started appearing, I really didn't see them as a rival to Bannatyne Fitness. I thought we operated in different markets: there had always been the old fashioned 'spit and sawdust' gyms where bodybuilders worked out with old equipment without the need for a pool (or in some cases even changing rooms); I thought the new low-cost operators were in competition with those clubs, not Bannatyne's or Esporta or David Lloyd. They were gyms, we were health clubs. However, as the financial crisis deepened, we started to feel their impact.

In the early days of Bannatyne Fitness, we developed a very strict set of criteria that a location had to meet before we would open a club there. We would do things like a drive-time analysis to see how many people lived within a ten-minute drive (which is about the maximum we've learned people are willing to drive to the gym), and we'd see which other operators were in the area. This meant that a lot of the time, we were able to open a club in a town or suburb where we really didn't have any competition. If someone in the area wanted to join a health club, we would often be the only choice. Of course we were still in competition with rival operators, as some people might choose to join a different club nearer their work rather than their home, but the fact is, we had a number of clubs that didn't have a direct competitor on their doorstep. Often it was only in big city centres that we had the kind of competition where a member had a choice between us and a comparable health-club operator. And with low-cost operators entering the market, those members were about to get a lot more choice.

At first we weren't too worried as our research showed that the people most attracted to low-cost gyms were under 30. This gave us a lot of comfort – only a third of our members are under 30. However, we had some city-centre clubs with a younger demographic, and they were potentially vulnerable.

Another reason we weren't worried at first was because quite a few operators had moved into the low-cost gym sector only to disappear as quickly as they arrived. I've already talked about Nuyuu, which had one of the daftest business models I've ever heard of: they knew that operating swimming pools was expensive so they planned to take over struggling clubs, fill in the pools and use that space for more gym equipment, in the hope of doubling their memberships.

They would have been better off renting office space, which would have been much cheaper and wouldn't have needed such expensive alterations. And how they thought they'd hold on to all their existing customers in that scenario is beyond me. No wonder they went under.

Since then, however, a few operators have found a model that seems to be working for them. The best-known is probably Pure Gym. They keep their costs low by only offering the basic minimum of equipment; they don't do classes and they don't have pools or saunas and steam rooms, just cardiovascular and resistance equipment. They also don't employ very many staff. Most of the people working on their premises tend to be freelance fitness instructors who have to work ten hours free to earn the right to then sell their services to members. I'm not even entirely sure if that's legal, but I presume it must be.

Members can only join online, and they gain entry by typing in their email address and a code. This means Pure Gym doesn't need sales or reception staff. Most low-cost gyms operate with a maximum of one member of staff on duty, and the 24-hour clubs won't have anyone on the premises between 10pm and 8am. It's no wonder then that some can charge as little as £8 a month. I estimate about a third of our clubs now have a low-cost rival within a few minutes' walk, and in places like Manchester and Birmingham we've had to adapt to survive.

We always knew that there would be some people who would prefer a cheap gym-only deal, no matter how superior our offering was. If they were never that bothered about the pool and the classes anyway, we had to accept that we would lose them to low-cost operators. However, we were also losing members who just wanted to try out the low-cost option, though when their sub-£10 fee was doubled after a year, a good percentage of them came back. I wasn't surprised: I'd heard lots of stories about homeless people taking out memberships for £8 a month and turning up with their sleeping bags after 8pm when there were no staff on the premises. They would then have a shower in the morning before the lone member of staff started their day at 8am. It's great if you have nowhere else to stay – it works out at 27p per night for bed and shower – but it doesn't make for the nicest of environments to spend your leisure time in.

Even though many of our members came back after 12 months, low-cost gyms continued to have an impact on our business. However, I've always believed that a competitor makes you stronger – Usain Bolt breaks world records because he's got Asafa Powell and Yohan Blake pushing him to go faster – so I started looking for ways to turn the situation to our advantage. If we were smart I knew we could learn things from low-cost gyms that would ultimately improve our business. We couldn't go as low as them on price, but that didn't mean we couldn't compete.

We started by focusing on Manchester, where we have three clubs, one of which was already losing money. We knew if we didn't make changes we would have to shut it down. I sat down with Nigel and we talked through our options. When we compared our clubs to the low-cost alternatives, it was clear we were offering a far superior prospect for potential members: besides the pool, we had better equipment, we offered a range of classes and we had staff on hand to deal with any problems. It was easy to persuade people we were worth more than a low-cost gym, but the question was how much more?

With one club losing money, we didn't have the luxury of taking our time to answer the question. Nigel and I kicked a few figures around and felt that £29 a month represented a bargain for members, and an acceptable baseline for us. We decided to let our sales team know that when potential members started to haggle and ask for a discount, they could drop the price to £29. We weren't quite in the Last Chance Saloon, but for me it still felt a bit like a roll of the dice. We were devaluing our brand and that instinctively felt wrong; but then if we didn't try it, I knew we faced the prospect of all our Manchester clubs losing money.

It's our policy that any member can use any other Bannatyne's health club in the country that charges the same as, or less than, their home club. That meant members in Manchester could use any of the three clubs for that reduced price. Even though it was a complete bargain, we didn't want to advertise the £29 deal because we'd have had thousands of members phoning up and asking to drop their £42 monthly direct debit down to the new price.

We decided to take a similar approach to pricing as some airlines do: the basic membership was competitive but, just as easyJet will charge for speedy boarding or seat allocation, we started charging for things that had previously been included. We no longer offered an automatic fitness assessment on joining: if members wanted one, they could pay extra. If they wanted a towel every time they came to work out, they could upgrade their membership to £36 a month. By tweaking our pricing structure, we limited some of the impact of dropping the price.

It's a fact of life that in city centres, health clubs tend to have higher churn rates (that is, the rate at which people cancel their memberships). This is for three reasons: firstly there's more competition; secondly many people work out near their job, and if they change jobs they also change gyms; and thirdly many city centre members are students who move on after two or three years. The impact of this meant that within a couple of years, most of our members were paying the reduced rate even though we hadn't advertised it.

Needless to say, I kept a very close eye on the monthly figures from Manchester and I kept expecting our EBITDA (that's Earnings Before Interest, Tax, Depreciation and Amortisation) and EBITDAR (the extra R is for Rent on our leasehold clubs) to take a hit. In 2011, all our earnings were impacted by the VAT hike, but in 2012 something remarkable happened – the profits in all our Manchester clubs went up. In 2010, our Quay Street club had been charging £42 a month and made £133,000 EBITDAR. In 2011 that dropped to £94,000 as members left for low-cost rivals and the VAT took a bite out of our profits, but in 2012 its figures jumped back up to £195,000.

It seemed crazy to me that we could make more from £29 memberships than £42 deals, but that's exactly what's happened. Clearly, £29 to use three clubs, three pools, three saunas and have a wider choice of classes is a very compelling proposition. In fact, it seems that the low-cost providers have actually become recruiters for us: they have tempted people who have never previously had gym memberships to sign up. And once people have the gym habit, a number of them have looked to upgrade and they've come to us. The businesses that I thought were going to cause us problems have actually turned out to be a source of new members!

We've faced low-cost opposition in a few locations, but the answer hasn't always been to compete on price. There are some places where we are better off having 1,500 members paying £40 a month because we simply couldn't find 2,000 to pay us £30 a month. If we can't attract any more members, then there's no point in letting the fees fall.

However, in Birmingham and Blackpool we also took the decision to lower our prices and although this has been good for our EBITDA, I still worry that we might be devaluing the brand. The manager of our Birmingham Priory club is my son-in-law Anthony, so he's one of the managers I speak to most often. He tells me that since we dropped the prices, the sort of customer we're attracting has changed. More and more, he says, people are trying it on, trying to sneak in a friend without paying, or making complaints in the hope of getting money back. Thankfully Anthony is 6'4" (as I mentioned earlier) and not easily intimidated if people start creating a scene. It's very reminiscent of stories I've heard from low-cost operators who have had big problems with direct debits being denied: once you lower your thresholds, you start to attract more of the kinds of customers who create problems and take up staff time.

Anthony says that the atmosphere in the club has changed. He's not even sure if it *feels* like a Bannatyne's club any more, and I worry what members who have been with us for many years think about the changes. I recently did a workout in one of our Manchester clubs. I was using equipment next to two Russian bodybuilders covered in tattoos who were talking loudly to each other. It struck me how intimidating they might be for some of our older members. Then I noticed that one of them was using the lat pull-down the wrong way: he was bringing it down behind his head, which is no longer considered best practice, rather than in front. I mentioned it to one of our instructors, but he said the guys didn't speak English and he couldn't make himself understood.

There is always the risk that if you let the atmosphere change in one club, it will eventually affect other clubs too. As our membership structure allows members to use other clubs, members who are used to the look and feel of a Bannatyne club might visit Anthony's club while they're in Birmingham and wonder if they're in the right place. And if the staff in Birmingham start to experience different problems from staff in other clubs, might that create internal tensions between clubs? When you have a chain of premises, when you have a brand, it's important to maintain consistency.

We are now considering whether we need to create our own economy brand. We'll never be as cheap as people like Pure Gym because our clubs have pools, but we could strip back some of our services, reduce staff and create a mid-level brand.

EIGHTEEN

Unfair Advantages

I don't have a problem with low-cost gyms offering cheaper memberships than Bannatyne's. What I do have a bit of a problem with is that they have what I see as an unfair advantage created by our government. It's not just the fact that they have smaller premises and fewer staff that keeps their costs down – government policy actually gives them a helping hand that isn't extended to us.

VAT is a tax on turnover, not profit (even businesses that are losing money have to pay their VAT every quarter). This means that the VAT increase has had a far bigger impact on us than it has on our low-cost rivals. Let's just say (to keep the maths simple) that we charge £40 a month and a low-cost rival charges £20. Let's also say that we offer what I'm going to call 'employee services' – things like classes, or inductions, or just someone on hand who can give you change for the vending machine if you need it – which are worth £20 a month. Both companies hand over 20% of their fees in VAT, so we pay £8 and the low-cost company pays £4. That means we're left with £12, while they get to keep £16.

Never in my career have I had to consider the impact of VAT or National Insurance on my business when making strategic decisions. But at 20%, the VAT rate is putting such pressure on our business that it's actually driving some of our choices. The tax tail is wagging the dog, so to speak, but the government doesn't seem to realise that the only way for companies to offset the high VAT is to employ fewer staff.

It's not just us, and not just the health-club sector, that's affected. Everyone must have noticed the arrival of self-service checkouts in shops, which mean that supermarkets now employ one person supervising ten tills rather than having ten people working on the checkouts. On a recent visit to Kings Cross train station, I purchased my rail ticket via the self service ticket machine, then went to WH Smith's where I paid for my purchases by way of a self service till, then went to look for a restaurant with table service but all 'restaurants' were counter service only. If all businesses follow the Pure Gym template, then unemployment is going to rise. At Bannatyne Fitness we're already investigating the possibility of installing fingerprint technology instead of employing receptionists: there must be thousands of business owners up and down the country making similar calculations.

For most businesses, their biggest cost has always been their staff. That's why there are usually so many job losses when a company changes hands: cutting staff has the biggest impact on reducing costs. Yet the government seems to want to make it even more expensive for businesses to employ people and doesn't seem to realise this will inevitably lead to fewer people being employed. When the government brings in pensions that force employers to make a contribution, this impacts disproportionately on the businesses that employ the largest number of people. In the health-club sector, this is effectively a tax on us that our low-cost rivals don't need to pay. To me, the situation is comparable to the non-dom scandals: I'm competing with companies that don't have to pay as much tax as me, and yet I'm the one creating the employment.

The crazy thing is that it's counterproductive: if companies like mine lay off staff, and competing companies don't hire so many people, then they won't be paying tax and we won't be paying employer's National Insurance contributions. What's the government going to do then? Put VAT up to 25%?

I feel strongly that all businesses should compete on a level playing field. I think most people feel the same, which is why there has been such a fuss in recent years about Starbucks having an unfair advantage over Costa Coffee, or Waterstones paying tax on its profits while Amazon sneaks them offshore. The thing that regulators and legislators haven't quite cottoned on to is that the more unfair we think our tax arrangements are, the more likely it is that we will start to question what exactly they are spending our money on.

Bannatyne Fitness collects £15 million a year in VAT on behalf of the Treasury. We also pay employer's National Insurance contributions, and through PAYE put millions more in income tax into the government coffers. I would love to have a politician tell me where all that money goes. When the Coalition came to power they said they were going to reduce costs and increase efficiency, but then they began to do things like spending millions on the Leveson Inquiry into press standards and deciding not to implement its recommendations! It was a complete waste of my money, your money and every taxpayer's money. Then they spent millions on a referendum in the Falkland Islands to find out what we already knew – that 98% of the islanders wanted to remain British. At a time when people in the UK are using food banks, you do find yourself questioning what the government is doing with all the money we give them.

I have no ideological problem with paying my taxes whatsoever, and I support any move that sees tax-avoidance loopholes closed. I believe the non-dom arrangements should be changed and it should become a rule that money earned in the UK is taxed in the UK. I think there is an argument, though, for saying that our tax rates are too high. Since the financial crisis hit, both governments have played around with the top rate of tax: Labour raised it to 50% from 40% before the Coalition reduced it to 45%. Like a lot of entrepreneurs, I don't take a salary out of my company so I am not personally hugely affected by this particular change, but I think 50% is too high because when you add on National Insurance you're paying more than half: it's not so much that I think it's a disincentive, it just doesn't seem fair. In my opinion, the top rate should never be higher than 40%.

One of the best things about having a public profile is that politicians do occasionally listen to the things I say, and it's why I get asked to take part in programmes like *Question Time*. They're good opportunities for me to put the case for business, and because we now have so many career politicians who've never had a job in the real economy, it's more important than ever that I speak out when I get the chance.

For instance, I have been trying for many years to explain to politicians that business has been forced to waste too many of its resources on employment tribunals. So, I was obviously happy when the Coalition brought in rules that made it easier to sack bad employees. However, I don't think the legislation went far enough – I feel that companies should be able to pursue the employees who make frivolous claims for compensation to get their costs back. Over the years we've found that a shockingly high percentage of the employees who take us to a tribunal for unfair dismissal have done the same with a previous employer. For some of them, it's obviously like putting in a false insurance claim – if they try it on often enough they might get some money for nothing. I think if they knew they could be sued for wasting their employers' time, as well as robbing taxpayers of money, they might not do it again.

For the record, I think the worst policy of any party in the UK at the moment has to be the Scottish National Party's referendum on Scottish independence. Why are we spending all that money on the campaign, and why are we letting our politicians get distracted from the important issues facing the economy by something that will be a disaster if it happens when we're already broke? And it won't just be a disaster for Scotland; England and the rest of the UK will suffer too. An independent Scotland isn't going to make one single person's life any better, in fact it could make things worse for millions of us because the uncertainty will be bad for business. If entrepreneurs don't know what currency Scotland will be using, or what legislation it will be subject to, how can they invest? If Scots vote 'yes' in 2014 they will be opening the country up to years of speculation that will do enormous damage.

Even if the referendum didn't cost a penny I would still think it was a ridiculous idea. Some of my family still live in Scotland, but I don't feel Scottish – I feel British. Of course I have strong emotional ties to the place where I grew up, but I also have strong ties to the place where my children grew up – in England. Many Scots have family members living south of the border, and more rely on English companies for their employment: it just doesn't make sense to separate yourself off. I can't see how independence will help Scotland, but I can see the harm in taking money away from schools and hospitals and roads and giving it to yet another layer of bureaucracy. Any party that wants me to lend my voice to the 'no' campaign knows where to find me.

In the past, I've made no secret of the fact that I supported New Labour. I thought the party did great things for the country under Tony Blair and I was a fan of Gordon Brown's chancellorship. When the Coalition came in, I thought it was a good compromise because the Conservatives couldn't run wild with the Lib Dems to keep them in check. I also thought the Coalition would be good for business, but I was clearly wrong about that.

I was also wrong when I thought Labour would be a good

voice in opposition: they've got the wrong front-bench team. The disaster started when Ed Miliband decided to fight his brother for the leadership. I don't think the public likes it when brothers fight, and to win elections you've got to be liked. I've heard a lot of people say that Ed Balls would make a good Chancellor, but he comes across as such a Rottweiler: it doesn't matter if your policies are brilliant if the voters don't find you likeable.

These days I don't support an individual party. I've had approaches from all sides but I don't have faith in any of them. That's not to say that I don't rate certain politicians – I still think Michael Fallon, with whom I launched Just Learning, is an incredibly decent guy; and William Hague, whom I've met a few times, is straightforward, intelligent and good company. In fact I think Hague could be a good prime minister and Michael Fallon should replace George Osborne: he has made too many mistakes as chancellor to keep his job.

But my opinion of the Conservatives isn't helped by the fact that they have on their front bench someone who is, in my opinion, the most repulsive man that has ever entered into politics. Kenneth Clarke earned millions of pounds as a director of British American Tobacco, a company that earns money selling single cigarettes to kids in Africa. I made a documentary on the subject and was appalled by Clarke's attitude to the company's practice. So long as he is in the Cabinet, I would be reluctant to vote Conservative at the next election, though I don't rule it out.

I will vote for the party that has the best policies to help entrepreneurs, and when I meet politicians I am happy to set out the changes that would secure my support. The more that bureaucracy can be simplified, the more it will encourage people to try setting up on their own. And some of the people starting small businesses today will be major employers in the future, so it's important that the state supports their efforts. After all, it's entrepreneurs that create growth and create wealth, the two things we need to start paying down the national debt.

But the first change I want to see is a reduction in VAT. I know there are other businesses that aren't affected by the rise – my Den investment Electro Expo, for example, which can simply pass the cost on because it's a wholesaler – but for those businesses that sell to the public and who employ a lot of staff, the 20% rate is disastrous. It's bad for business to have it so high, which means it's bad for the economy, which ultimately means it's also bad for the country.

NINETEEN

Putting Things in Perspective

No matter how tough things got dealing with bankers and bureaucrats at work, I actually considered myself extremely lucky to be going through all that turmoil – I thought I was lucky to be alive. In January 2010, I had been due to visit Haiti with two of the charities I support, Scottish International Relief and UNICEF. I'd been due to fly out on 19 January, but on 12 January the country suffered one of the most devastating earthquakes in recorded history and the hotel we had been booked into collapsed. If we had travelled a week earlier – well, I wouldn't be writing this book.

As soon as news of the earthquake broke, UNICEF called to say they were cancelling the trip, as the priority was obviously now disaster relief rather than humanitarian support. I told them that as soon as it was sensible for the trip to be rescheduled, I was still keen to visit because Haiti would be needing even more help now.

I've been involved with SIR and UNICEF for two decades now. They are at extreme ends of the charitable sector – one is a tiny organisation run from a garden shed, and the other is world-famous and gets support from some very big names. Both charities do amazing work, and ensuring that I make enough profit to be able to continue to support their projects has been a real motivation for me throughout my career.

I eventually flew out to Haiti in January 2011 and my daughter Hollie came with me. In the same way that my kids have become interested in the family business as they've got older, they have also become increasingly curious about the charities that we support. They've grown up with me coming home from trips to Romanian orphanages, or schools in Malawi, and although my charity work has always been part of their lives, I think it was only as they got older that they really began to appreciate how much it means to me. Hollie said she wanted to learn more about what our Foundation does and how we help people. She and her sister Evie have already been to visit the orphanage I fund in Romania to learn how that works, and in April 2013 Hollie organised a charity ball at Charlton House hotel which raised £25,000 for the Bannatyne Charitable Trust. I think in the future she actually wants to work for the Foundation.

When Hollie asked if she could come with me to Haiti I was in two minds as to whether I should say yes. On the one hand, it would be a fantastic opportunity for her to learn about the work of the foundation, but on the other hand Haiti is not the safest of places and had recently acquired the label of rape capital of the world.

You might think that in a country devastated by an earthquake and then ravaged by a cholera outbreak, the survivors would somehow be motivated to look out for one another. Yet the rape statistics indicate how desperate people become when their livelihoods, as well as their homes and families, are taken from them.

I decided to hire an armed bodyguard for Hollie and made a few phone calls before we flew to Port-au-Prince. We met the bodyguard, who had been recommended by a contact of mine, at Miami airport, where we had a connecting flight. I took him to one side because I wanted to be absolutely sure that he knew what he was being hired to do.

'Your job is to look after Hollie. Just Hollie. If we get in trouble, you just get Hollie out.' Then I added: 'If you come back for me I'll kill you because that's not your job. Your job is only to protect Hollie, no one else.'

Flying into a country that's been flattened by an earthquake is an unnerving experience. You can see from the air how much has been lost and you can spot the regimented tent cities, and you know as the plane gets lower that the statistics you've read about in newspapers are going to be replaced by heartbreaking sights you're never going to forget. One of my most striking memories of that descent was realising that we had hardly seen any fields. If there was no agriculture, how was Haiti supposed to feed itself? I remember when I first visited Romania just after Ceauşescu had been overthrown I said to myself, 'It's going to take 50 years to sort this place out.' With Haiti, I found myself wondering if it would ever be possible.

When we got off the plane, we saw hundreds and hundreds of people lining the perimeter fence of the airport. People were just standing there, staring at the planes and the passengers. Amongst the crowd there was a single white face, and it was someone I thought I recognised.

We made our way into the terminal building and were instantly surrounded by people in uniform who wanted to carry our bags. Obviously I have no problem tipping people who desperately need a dollar, but given what we'd heard about crime I didn't want to let go of my bag. When we made it to the other side of the building, there was a 4×4 waiting for us, and that's when I saw the man I had recognised again. Hollie recognised him too: it was Sean Penn. He was in the country without any entourage, or any publicity, quietly lending support to the rebuilding programme. We nodded an acknowledgement to each other.

Hollie and I were travelling with the founder of Scottish International Relief, Magnus MacFarlane-Barrow, who is one of the most remarkable people I have ever met. Magnus started SIR from the shed at the bottom of his dad's garden in Argyll. Originally he just collected unwanted clothes and drove them across Europe to Bosnia after the war there, but when he realised that people wanted to donate more than clothes, he started SIR.

I first met Magnus at a charity event in 2001, and when he found out that I had supported projects in Romania, he invited me to a town called Târgu Mureş where SIR had built homes for children rescued from Ceauşescu-era orphanages.

I use the term 'orphanage' loosely, as most of the children weren't orphans; their mothers had simply been encouraged to give up their children into the care of the state. After Ceauşescu was overthrown in 1989, western media started to expose the scandal of children kept in the most appalling circumstances – chained to their cots with no one to talk to them, or cuddle them, or even change them when they soiled themselves. The physical and psychological damage done to these children was immense. I had been so shocked by the images on the news that I started fund-raising for a local charity. That led to my first visit to Romania in 1995 and I'd subsequently visited again with UNICEF.

When I saw what Magnus and Scottish International Relief were doing on such a small budget, I became utterly committed to helping him. I funded the building of a third home – which I was incredibly honoured to find out Magnus had called Casa Bannatyne – and have been meeting the running costs ever since.

I have watched with admiration as Magnus has gone from project to project, always with the same dedication and sense of purpose. The programme that SIR is best known for now is Mary's Meals, an amazing idea that is having a massive impact on communities as far apart as Malawi, the Philippines and Ecuador. Magnus had discovered that lots of schools had been built but were lying empty and becoming derelict because not enough children were attending. Mary's Meals deals with this by providing one simple meal a day to children – at school. Knowing that their children will be fed is a big incentive for parents to send them to be educated. Mary's Meals makes sure the children get enough nutrition to be healthy and to be able to pay attention in class. It's easy to see how this very simple idea can end up having a huge positive impact on an entire community.

Mary's Meals now feeds over 750,000 children every day. That's three-quarters of a million kids spared the consequences of malnutrition. Three-quarters of a million kids getting an education. And when they grow up, that will be 750,000 families lifted a little further out of poverty. It is a phenomenal achievement, and it only takes £10 to feed a child for a year – a small price for such life-changing results.

We were in Haiti to see what it would take to start offering Mary's Meals to kids there, but it quickly became apparent that the devastation was of a magnitude that I had not witnessed before. How can you feed kids in school if their school has been completely destroyed? As we were taken from one heartbreaking situation to another by a contact of Magnus's, I started to think that I shouldn't just be funding Mary's Meals. I started to think that I also needed to build a school.

It's hard to explain just how much the charity work I do means to me; I can talk about how it feels good to know you are helping people, and I know that it also means a lot to our staff and our members that the company does so much for charity, but for me there is something more going on. I'm not sure I have the words to express it clearly, but I feel *protected* when I am in the most desolate and dangerous places.

I've written previously about the many coincidences that have occurred in my life because of my charity work. I have been persuaded by Christian friends that there have been so many of these coincidences that they can't all be explained away. I'm not a particularly religious person, but I have had some profound experiences when I'm in places like Haiti, as if He's there with me. I never feel in any danger. I feel *safe*.

Magnus is one of life's gentle giants. Over 6ft tall, he's very softly spoken and has the ability to talk to people in a way that makes them feel understood. He is absolutely fearless; he just walks into the most dangerous places, and I have no qualms about following him. He also has a very strong Christian faith; I don't know if that's the source of his determination, or his humility, but he puts himself in situations that most people would shy away from. He truly is the most inspirational person I have ever met.

SIR was building a partnership in Haiti with another charity called Hands Together. We were shown round by Father Tom from Hands Together. He took us to see some of the most distressing sights I have ever seen. Then, after several hours of driving through one flattened settlement after another, he took us to visit a school. Every single child was wearing a clean, pressed school uniform. I'd seen something similar in Romania years before: in desperate, devastated communities, parents will do everything they can to make sure their children get an education. They put the uniforms under the mattress before they go to sleep – just like my mum did with our uniforms – and will go without so their children can have shoes so they can walk to school. Amongst the dust and the ruins, the sight and sound of brightly dressed, noisy children is the sort of thing that gives you hope in an otherwise heartbreaking place.

With Father Tom's help, we started making enquiries about building a school, but the situation in Haiti was so chaotic, and the construction industry in such demand, that we agreed a first step would be to add a wing onto an existing school. It was a great honour to be in a position to help.

I've been involved in enough charity projects now to know that good intentions don't always create good outcomes. Father Tom told us a story about ten houses that had been built in Haiti with charitable donations. The community had decided between themselves which families were most deserving of the accommodation, but when the charity went back a month later, they found ten completely different families living there. Men with machetes had arrived, evicted the families and started renting the houses out to the highest bidder. In places where there is no effective rule of law, small charities need to choose their projects very carefully.

In contrast, we also saw a truly inspirational example of the difference entrepreneurs can make in a disaster zone. Whereas charities have a responsibility to their donors to spend money in a certain way – and they sometimes have stakeholders and boards that need to be consulted before money can be released – an entrepreneur can make a decision there and then and put booster rockets under a project to get it done quickly.

Denis O'Brien is an Irish entrepreneur who has made billions from the telecoms industry. His company, Digicel, had installed mobile-phone masts across Haiti and when he visited the country he saw that one of the few sources of foreign income had been cut off: before the earthquake, cruise ships used to dock for a couple of hours and passengers would get off and buy trinkets and food in the marketplace. The earthquake flattened the marketplace and so the boats stopped docking.

Of course it wasn't just the tourists who used the market. Its loss impacted on every trader in the area, so O'Brien took it upon himself to rebuild it; now traders have rebuilt their businesses, and everyone benefits from the additional revenue of a bit of tourism. If Haiti could also build a casino or a hotel complex, it might really change the economic future, but for the moment, replacing homes, schools and hospitals will take priority.

Knowing that entrepreneurs can bring so many benefits helps you to deal with the inevitable guilt that you feel when you visit somewhere like Port-au-Prince. Although the hotel we were staying in was very basic and just a few yards from one of the biggest rubbish tips in the country (along with some of the biggest rats) there was always food for us. Sometimes there wasn't milk to go with the cereal, but we could never really shake off the feeling that there were people who needed the food more than we did.

After spending a few days with Magnus, Hollie and I transferred into the care of UNICEF. Wherever we went, we saw countless people just sitting at the side of streets, people with no money, no houses, no work and nowhere to go.

UNICEF took us to one of the tented villages that exist all over the country. We'd seen them on the news but the images on TV do not prepare you for seeing them up close. And hearing them. And smelling them. And yet many, many people are desperate to move into the tented villages, not just because they are safer than the chicken-coop houses in the country's slums, but because the people in tents are first in line to get a house when they're finally built.

We were introduced to lots of people that day, and they all had heartbreaking stories to tell. One couple stand out in my memory, though. Inside their tent we found another tent.

'What's that tent for?' I asked through an interpreter.

'That's where the baby sleeps,' they told me. 'It zips up. The rats won't get him in there.'

There just isn't much you can say in a situation like that. All you can do is make sure that when you get home you don't forget, and that you keep making funds available for organisations like UNICEF.

As we were leaving the tent village, we saw a group of boys playing. At first we thought they had a small football, then we wondered if it was a puppy, and finally, when we got closer, we realised they were playing with a rat.

'That will be cooked for dinner tonight,' our guide said.

It can be overwhelming, visiting places like that camp. The problems are so complex and so numerous that it would be easy to feel helpless. But working with Magnus gives me hope. I've seen how, project by project and year by year, lives can be transformed. In Romania, for example, many of the children in Târgu Mureş have grown up, got educated and started careers – something that seemed impossible when we first started working there.

A couple of years ago Adela, one of the girls who had grown up in Casa Bannatyne, got in touch and asked if I would give her away at her wedding. I can't tell you what a fantastic feeling that was. I had known some of the kids there since they were five; I had seen them overcome enormous disadvantages (most of them were HIV-positive, for example), and I felt extremely proud of what had been achieved in Târgu Mureş. That Adela had thought of me when planning her wedding made my heart swell with pride and my eyes fill with tears.

It was one of the most amazing days of my life. As 'father of the bride' there were all these odd rituals I had to take part in, even though I couldn't speak the language. At one point the oldest, ugliest woman in the town put on the wedding dress and I had to try to palm her off on the groom! When he refused to take her, I had to come back with Adela, and much of the rest of the day was also like appearing in a Romanian farce. It was wonderful to see Adela so happy, and it was an experience I will never forget.

The following day I went out for a drink with Ibi, the manageress of SIR's homes in Târgu Mureş. She took me to a coffee shop that her sons had opened, and while we were chatting, two teenagers popped their heads round the door then quickly left.

'Why did they go?' I asked Ibi.

'They said the place was full of old people!'

I thought that was one of the best things I had ever heard: when I had first visited Târgu Mureş there hadn't been *anywhere* to go for a drink. Now there were so many choices that those teenagers wanted to find their own crowd. It highlighted the kinds of changes that can happen in the space of a generation. Târgu Mureş still has a long way to go, but it has already come so far. I hope that if I go back to Haiti in the future I'll see similarly remarkable progress. When I think of what a difference a generation fed by Mary's Meals can make, I have hundreds of reasons to be hopeful.

TWENTY

The Final Blow

The lesson you learn from visiting a disaster zone like Haiti is that life can change in an instant. None of us know what's round the corner, or what will happen tomorrow: you might fall in love, or you might fall over and break your neck. The reality is that – despite the comfort and security of modern life – anything can happen to anyone at any time.

When we got back from Haiti at the end of January 2011, life became its usual blur of business meetings and family events. Whenever we got the chance, Joanne and I would take Emily and Tom to our villa in France and most nights we'd either be joined by my older kids, or her parents or her sister and brother-in-law.

It was a particularly special time for the Bannatynes as my eldest daughter Abigail was pregnant with her second child, and we were all looking forward to welcoming a little brother for Ava. I think Tom and Emily got a big kick out of having a niece – it made them feel very grown up.

Austin was born on 6th May, and not long after I had been to visit him, I had a meeting in London ahead of filming getting underway on the ninth series of *Dragons' Den*. The company had bought a flat in London a few years previously. My media work meant I was in London a lot, and when Nigel and Chris needed to meet with bankers and brokers, those meetings almost always happened in London. We had been spending so much on hotel rooms that it had made financial sense to buy somewhere. It was a very nice flat in the heart of Covent Garden but it never felt like home. It was somewhere for meetings and crashing late at night, but it was nevertheless a lot better than being in a hotel room for days on end while we were filming.

By the ninth series, I really felt that we knew how to make a good show. I'm not saying we could do it on autopilot, but we all knew what was required of us, and we all worked hard to make the show as good as it had been at the start. I felt like we had a good rhythm going, and we were having a lot of fun. But as I was saying, you just never know when life is going to change.

It was at the start of a new week, and Peter and I were catching up between pitches in the car park at Pinewood. We have to turn our phones off while we're filming, so the first thing we do when we get outside is switch them on and wait for the inevitable bleeps and rings.

There was a text from Joanne. My hands started to shake as I read it.

She said she had filed for divorce in the High Court and that the petition would be waiting for me when I returned to the flat.

I couldn't speak. I just showed the text to Peter. He looked as shocked as I felt. I couldn't take it in, in part because I couldn't believe that after 18 years together she didn't tell me in person.

Peter's home is not too far from Pinewood, and he immediately offered for me to stay with him if that would help. I felt like my head was going to explode with the confusion, but Peter was great and helped keep me focused.

The next thing I did was phone Nigel: as well as being my chief executive, Nigel is also a very good friend. I instantly knew that if Joanne was serious Nigel had to know about it: finances were tight and finding the funds for a settlement might be difficult.

'This is a bit out the blue, isn't it?' Nigel asked. 'Did you know it was on the cards?'

I didn't. I honestly didn't. I know people always think that you would know if your wife or husband was planning for a divorce, but I really, truly didn't have a clue. I knew the past couple of weeks had been a bit awkward, but I didn't have a single brain cell that had thought this was about to happen.

The awkward phase had started a few weeks before. Joanne had come in to the office to have lunch with me as I was about to go to London and we wouldn't see each other for a few days. She had a session booked with her personal trainer so we met in the café of the health club right next to our HQ. Over lunch, Joanne told me that she wanted to get more involved in the business again and to work on a specific project we had underway. Since we already had experts employed to handle all aspects of this – including design – I told her that this wasn't really possible.

Nothing more was said about it. We finished lunch, she went off for her training session and I went back to the office before getting on the train to London. But while I was still in the office, Joanne sent a text to her sister – only she sent it to me by mistake. In it she said some things about me which I found extremely hurtful and derogatory.

I really didn't know what to do. I finished up at the office and walked to the station which is about 10 minutes away. I usually get quite a lot of work done on the train but I just couldn't concentrate on anything. I couldn't pretend I hadn't received that message, so I texted back and by the time I got to London I had received several more texts that left me feeling confused and angry.

When I got to the flat I realised that I didn't want to go back home. I couldn't. Not unless I got an apology or an explanation for the things that had been said. After a few days, we talked again and Joanne finally admitted that she had been angry with me when she'd sent the first text, but she explained that she didn't feel that way now. It had just been a heat of the moment thing because I'd rejected the idea of her getting involved with the business.

It wasn't enough. I felt I needed an apology before I could return home. It was relatively easy for me to stay in London as I had enough clothes there and, thanks to my BlackBerry, I can pretty much work anywhere anyway.

For the next couple of weeks, Joanne and I communicated by text, only speaking when I called to talk to the kids. I kept expecting to come back to the flat in the evening and find her there, or for a letter or a card to have arrived. One night I let myself in to find a massive bouquet of flowers on the table. My heart leapt. *She's here*, I thought! But when I read the card it turned out they were from a production company thanking me for working with them.

Since I didn't think I had done anything wrong, I didn't see why I should be the one to build bridges. And so I stayed in London until *Dragons' Den* started filming. And in all that time, I really, honestly believed that she would send me a sign. She'd apologise, or she'd phone me, she would say she was really sorry and make up some excuse to explain why she really didn't mean the things she'd said. That was what I was hoping for. In fact, she was thinking divorce.

TWENTY-ONE

It *is* About the Money

Joanne and I had met when she worked as a nurse for Quality Care Homes. When I split up from my first wife, Gail, Joanne was one of the people who was thoughtful enough to ask how I was and to invite me along to things. By the time Gail and I had divorced, Joanne and I were an item.

Joanne and I were very compatible, despite the fact that she is 17 years younger than me. We both shared a love of business, we loved working together, we both wanted kids together . . . honestly, from the fact that she understood my need to always have my phone on, to her love of work-outs in the club, Joanne and I really understood each other. I fell deeply and completely in love with her, and for a number of years we were together 24 hours a day. There aren't many couples I know that can do that without falling out. We never did. We were mates and we got on great.

There was, however, one area where we had different

attitudes, and that was spending money. When I look back now, I can't say I didn't notice that she was extravagant.

It never seemed to matter to either of us that we weren't married. Even when we celebrated our tenth anniversary together, even when our second child was born, it was a subject that neither of us gave a lot of thought. We lived together, we had kids together – why did we need a piece of paper? I honestly think that if we had never got married, Joanne and I would still be together.

Things weren't always perfect and there was a period in 2004 and 2005 when I was in London a lot. I had started making *Dragons' Den* and I was also being offered the occasional acting job (I had small parts in a few short films and a couple of TV series). I had bought a tiny flat in London which wasn't much bigger than a hotel room, and so it became convenient for me to spend more time away from Joanne and the kids.

It was the first time in our relationship – we'd been together for twelve or thirteen years at this point – that we drifted apart. But for me it was also an exciting time: I was getting a lot of interesting offers to take part in TV shows, or invites to celebrity events. To her credit, Joanne realised that I needed to enjoy it all – I had worked flat out for 25 years and she felt I deserved to reap the rewards of success. Meanwhile, she was at home with two small kids and our lives just diverged. After a few months we started to wonder what kind of relationship we had, and a few months after that we agreed to separate.

Although we weren't married, I recognised that I had a responsibility to look after Joanne financially. We agreed that

I would buy her a house – which would be in her own name – and make her a monthly payment to cover all the expenses for the kids. I thought it was more than enough for her to live a good life and for the kids not to go without.

We never fell out. It was a difficult adjustment but we negotiated everything amicably between us. She bought a modest house on the Wynyard Park estate near Billingham which was famous locally for being where lots of Newcastle United players had their mansions. Not long after Joanne bought her house, I bought one just round the corner – I wanted Tom and Emily to be able to come and visit me without needing to get a lift.

For a year or so, we both started seeing other people. Although Emily and Tom lived with Joanne, I saw them all the time and was always on hand if they needed me. I got on with running the businesses and with my TV career, while Joanne opened a little business of her own – running a boutique in the village of Yarm with her sister. Life seemed pretty good, but I really missed our family holidays. We had always enjoyed lots of holidays – it's a luxury I've always been happy to pay for – and I also realised spending time at the villa wasn't nearly as much fun on my own.

I told Joanne that I wanted to take Emily and Tom to France with me, but she said she was a bit unsure about me being there on my own with them. After all there's a pool – I could be indoors with one of them leaving the other unsupervised. I tried not feel insulted that she thought I could be so irresponsible, but was really quite happy when she suggested a compromise – that she should come too.

Spending time as a family again, just the four of us, was wonderful. It felt like we had never been apart, and one night after the kids had gone to bed, we couldn't deny our feelings for each other any longer. When we got back to the UK, we took things slowly as we didn't want Tom and Emily to get too excited. I carried on living round the corner, but we'd spend many nights together. We were LATs – Living Apart Together – and it worked out incredibly well.

However, our living arrangements meant friends were unsure exactly what the deal was, and I think we both felt a need to make a public declaration. Joanne dropped hints that maybe we should get married, and while we were on holiday in Barbados I finally proposed. Although I was sure she would say yes, I was still absolutely delighted when she did. I wanted to be married. It felt right. We felt ready. It was all going to be fine.

I left the wedding arrangements to Joanne. Apart from setting a budget – which was broken several times – all I had to do was put on a suit and turn up. To her credit, Joanne didn't spend a lot of money on venue hire. The company owned a warehouse round the back of our old HQ that had been the venue for Joanne's 40th birthday party, which had been a massive success. The place was big enough for hundreds of people, and because of the health club there was also parking for all of them, but the biggest bonus was that because it was nowhere near residential property we could make as much noise as we liked for as long as we liked. When I walked into the warehouse I couldn't believe it: Joanne had had the entire interior draped in white cloth and it was really quite beautiful. It was absolutely one of the best days of my life and when I said my vows, I meant them with all my heart.

Our financial arrangements didn't change. All that changed was that I moved into Joanne's house and sold mine. I also sold the little flat in London. Her house was smaller than mine, but it was the kids' home and they had friends who lived in the street. Neither Joanne or I wanted to uproot them.

I loved being married. I think it suited me. I was 57, I was successful, I was in love – it was absolutely the right thing to do. I don't regret it. What I do regret, with hindsight, is not signing a pre-nup. But I was too in love to have asked her, even if I had thought it was a good idea.

My best man, John Moreton, was one of several friends who had suggested getting an agreement drawn up.

I told him: 'I don't care, I've got to marry her – I'm madly in love.'

There have been many times since when I have wished that I took his advice.

In the years after the wedding I estimate I spent around £80,000 per annum taking us on holiday. South Africa, Barbados, skiing, and of course spending time in France. I loved flying the entire family – including my four older kids – business class and taking rooms in the best hotels. It was a complete luxury and one we all enjoyed. These were absolutely some of the best years of my life.

I'm always very happy to spend money on the people I love but there's absolutely no point in wasting it. Just because I can afford another pair of shoes, or another car, it doesn't mean I buy those things for myself. I don't like to spoil my kids, either. Joanne was different. If she saw something she liked, she invariably bought it, and I noticed that our expenditure was spiralling upwards. She wouldn't just buy things for herself – quite the contrary, she was extremely generous in buying things for friends and family – and this had become a way of life.

So when I stood in that car park with Peter Jones, shaking with disbelief, I knew it was going to be expensive.

TWENTY-TWO

The Benefit of Hindsight

A few years ago, a wealthy friend of mine started dropping hints that she had a new boyfriend.

'Well, let's meet him,' I said, half-thinking he might be a figment of her imagination because she'd been so reluctant to introduce him. But as the months went on it became quite clear that she was genuinely falling in love. 'It's getting pretty serious, isn't it about time we all met?'

Again it didn't happen. The next time I saw her, she had a big engagement ring on her hand. I congratulated her and insisted that it really was time I finally got to meet him. So she arranged a dinner for her friends to get together with her fiancé. I have to say I wasn't impressed. He was clearly a gigolo and he wasn't young enough or pretty enough to be worth her while.

'You have signed a pre-nup, haven't you?' I asked as I helped her on with her coat after dinner.

'Of course I have!' she laughed. 'I'm not stupid. If we split up, he's not getting more than a million. It's in black and white.'

So, fast forward a couple of weeks to the wedding. Well, to the day after the wedding to be precise, when my friend woke up to find that her husband – after consummating the marriage – had done a runner. There was a note on the pillow: it was the name and number of his divorce lawyer.

She was as humiliated as she was angry. She had been conned. She had fallen in love and he had only ever wanted money. Her instinct was to fight it. How dare he? I felt her anger, I really did, but I had to tell her she was probably better off paying the money. 'You'll only end up paying another million to a lawyer,' I said.

She wasn't going to lie down and take it – you don't get to be as successful as she is by giving in to bullies – so she spoke to several lawyers. They all told her the same thing: if she had the money don't fight it – just give him the million and walk away. Get a clean break and start over. In the end that's what she did. Looking back I wished we had a pre-nup too. I think Joanne would have signed one, if I'd asked her, but I had been too in love to even consider it.

A member of the *Dragons' Den* production team rushed out to tell us they were ready for the next pitch. I went onto autopilot; I asked simple questions and felt relieved when I remembered to declare myself out. With each pitch, I felt more and more detached, less and less sure of what I had said. All I could think about was the text from Joanne. I was devastated. Stunned. I remember looking at somebody who had come in to pitch to us and being vaguely aware that Peter was speaking, then Deborah said something and I realised I had no idea who the person was or what their product was. I just stood up and walked off and went and cried somewhere. They finished filming with just four dragons.

Somehow they managed to cut and edit the programme without me saying anything, or sometimes they'd get me back in the chair to say a line or two, but I really didn't know what was happening that afternoon. By the end of the day, everyone knew about my text from Joanne, and the entire production team was incredibly sensitive and supportive. After filming, a driver took me back to the flat in Covent Garden where I found the divorce petition. There hadn't really been any part of me that thought Joanne was joking, but seeing the actual documents was incredibly painful. And then when I started to read them I realised I was shaking. She had hired Fiona Shackleton, the lawyer who had represented Paul McCartney in his divorce. She did such a good job that Heather Mills was reported to have thrown a jug of water over her when their settlement was reached.

I don't remember much more about that night, either because I was in so much shock or because I drank too much, but the next day I took the petition in to the studios and showed it to Peter.

'I'm going to call my lawyer,' he said, 'If she's got Fiona Shackleton, you need a top London lawyer too. My guy's great, leave it with me.'

I was happy and grateful for any offer of help: I really wasn't capable of doing anything myself. Peter put in his call and we went in to start filming. It was no better than the day before. I couldn't concentrate. I couldn't keep any facts or figures in my head. I was going through the motions of being a dragon, sitting in the chair, looking at the person standing in front us, but I wasn't seeing anything. I didn't know what was going on half the time.

At one point that week, someone came in with a caravan cushion business, and half way through their pitch I started thinking 'I have no idea what they're talking about.' And then Hilary made an offer for half the money, and I found myself saying that I would match Hilary's offer. I had no idea what the business model was. None. If you look at series nine now (and there's usually an episode on Dave every day) you can see there are lots of pitches where I declare myself out without giving a reason. I honestly don't know if that's because I didn't give a reason, or because they edited in footage from a different pitch. It must have been a nightmare for the editors.

At the next break in filming, Peter came to see me. He'd just got off the phone to his lawyer. I could tell from his face that he didn't have good news.

'There's a conflict.'

'What does that mean?'

'Joanne went to see the firm. She spent over an hour with one of the top people there.'

I didn't really understand why that was significant.

'They think there's a conflict of interest. They don't want to take you on.'

I was later told that Joanne had visited other divorce lawyers in London, which meant I was blocked from getting representation from them. If this was true then maybe Joanne had been planning divorce for some time.

TWENTY-THREE

Rock Bottom

The next few weeks are difficult for me to piece together. In a way I am very grateful this happened while we were filming. *Dragons' Den* gave me a reason to get up in the morning and made it easier for me to keep putting one foot in front of the other. A car came to pick me up in the morning, and throughout the day I had people telling me where to go and what to do, and many of them were kind enough to make sure I was eating properly. Then, at the end of the day, a car would come and take me home again. That structure was incredibly helpful.

My overriding emotion at that time was anger. If I had been unfaithful or abusive I would have understood, but I just didn't know how my wife could have been thinking about something like this without me knowing. I thought about the lazy Sunday mornings in bed, the trips out with the kids, the holidays to Barbados – suddenly every happy memory I had of our marriage was tainted by this rage that it was all a lie.

My mind kept turning over and over past events, looking for clues of her unhappiness or signs that she was withdrawing from the relationship. As I looked back, I realised there were a few incidents of evasive or dismissive behaviour that now made a lot more sense to me.

Eventually I found a lawyer in the north-east who started preparing my response to the petition (it wasn't long before he was outgunned by Shackleton and I had to find representation from a London lawyer who could withstand the onslaught), and when the paperwork started going back and forth, it felt like there was an orchestrated campaign to destroy me.

But of course, it wasn't just me that was threatened by the divorce: when your wealth is tied up in a business as mine is, it is impossible not to equate the demands of the settlement with the cost to the business. Over the next few months, the financial demands on me increased: not only did I have my own legal bills, but I had to pay Joanne's too. And this was on top of finding the money for a new house so I had a place to call home.

Divorce lawyers never tell you how much the divorce is going to cost you upfront and many clients lose sight of the fact that the legal costs will come out of the matrimonial assets – money you could share with your ex if it didn't get gobbled up by your lawyers. Let's say a man (for the sake of this example we'll assume the man is the wealthy one) is worth £20 million and they agree to divide the assets 50:50. Those assets will be divided after the costs have been deducted, so if a divorce costs £4 million then that leaves assets of £16 million which will then be split equally. The wife gets £8 million and the divorce has effectively cost her £2 million. But lawyers don't explain that very clearly as it would probably have a negative impact on their fees.

I found the process completely overwhelming and I felt powerless as our marriage was reduced to legal arguments and points of law. As the paperwork mounted up I started to feel beaten up. That's the best way I can describe it. Of course the divorce process is hugely costly but the psychological effect is much worse. Every time saw a document, or received another call about some petty discrepancy, I felt so fucking sad. I was no longer able to commit funds to charitable causes I cared about, and this broke my heart. I started sinking rapidly. Anxiety and anger turned into depression and I didn't know how to get myself out it. Suicide began to feel like a possible option.

The first couple of weeks of June that year were just awful. I felt everything I loved was being taken away from me. It all seemed so unnecessary. I would often think about my first divorce from Gail where we decided everything between us round the kitchen table. If it hadn't been for the example of my first divorce, I would probably agree that divorce is always bitter, as it's designed to pit couples against each other. But I knew it didn't have to be that way and that knowledge made me feel desperately sad. I would sit in the flat in London and bawl my eyes out.

At some point in those two weeks – which were the lowest I think I have ever been – I reached out on Twitter and said (and I only remember this because it was reported in the papers) that suicide was on my mind. It wasn't long after that that Hollie turned up on my doorstep. We sat up all night, and then the next night. After that, my elder daughters took it in turns to make sure I was all right.

On more than one occasion, I got up in the morning and wandered down to the kitchen to find two or three empty wine bottles. It would take me a couple of minutes to realise I had been the only one at home the night before. I knew drinking so much wasn't healthy, but it was also one of the things that helped me cope. Of course, alcohol isn't just bad for your liver, it's poison for your brain too and I felt myself becoming more and more depressed.

There were a couple of times that summer when I was waiting at Darlington station for a train down to London. I don't know what the other people on the platform thought as they saw me there with tears streaming down my face, but the truth is I was thinking I could just end it all. The fast train would be coming through any minute and it would all be over. It honestly felt like it was the only way I could make the pain stop. I would start to have these strange thoughts about what would happen if I died. It's a terrible way to think but divorce can have that effect.

But then I would worry about what would be left for my kids, and with the economy in the state it's in, I thought I could make the company more valuable again and leave them a better inheritance. And then I realised that the divorce was reducing everything to numbers, to money, and I hated that. What mattered wasn't the amount, it was my kids. What mattered was that I was there for them.

The train whizzed past and I was still standing there.

TWENTY-FOUR

Going to Court

It probably won't surprise you to learn that Joanne and I stopped speaking. If I wanted to get a message to her, I had to ask Kim, my PA, to call Joanne's aunt Joan who would pass the information on.

Sadly, more often than not, Joanne and I were communicating through lawyers. The problem with that method of communication is that it is very, very expensive. It's been my experience that lawyers will take the piss if you give them half a chance: I still don't know what I got charged for every letter that was sent. I hadn't been overdrawn since the early days of Quality Care Homes, but by the end of the divorce I was back to living on credit cards.

To an outsider, I can see it must have looked like I had some influence over the situation. After all, I was rich, I lived in a bigger house than Joanne, I could afford the best lawyers. It's difficult to explain that from the moment the divorce proceedings started I felt like the victim. I felt bullied and all I could do was react to whatever was thrown at me.

I had no problem with making a financial settlement – I had done it very amicably with Gail all those years ago. My problem wasn't that I thought Joanne wasn't entitled to a substantial payment, my problem was with the method and the manner in which it was handled. With every letter, with every phone call, I just felt bullied and all I could do was take it.

On many occasions people asked me, 'Have you got a good lawyer?' But the thing I know now is that there is no such thing as a 'good' divorce lawyer. It's not like criminal law where a sharp barrister can make the difference between 'guilty' and 'not guilty'. The size of the settlement really only relates to the size of the matrimonial assets, not the quality of the argument you make. As one lawyer said to me, 'It doesn't matter if your wife sat at home and filed her nails every day for ten years and shagged the local football team, the starting point for any divorce is that both parties are entitled to half.'

What this means is that anyone who does not attempt an amicable settlement before employing hugely expensive lawyers is robbing themselves: all lawyers do is reduce the size of the bank balance that is soon to be divided. Certainly my first wife has never regretted our amicable settlement.

One of the people who really looked after me during this time was Noel Edmonds. I'd met him a few years previously at a party, and I got talking to him about *Deal or No Deal*. I was – I am – a really big fan of the show and I think he was a bit surprised how much I had to say on the subject. We talked for hours, and during the conversation we realised that we lived near each other in the south of France. He visited my villa, I went round to his, and we became very good friends. When he found out about the divorce, he invited me to stay with him and his wife Liz. He was great to talk to, and after a few days he said he had spoken to a few people and had found me a lawyer.

'The person you need right now is a lady called Liz Vernon. She works for a firm called Clintons.' He handed me a piece of paper. 'This is her number.'

I called Liz up and she seemed to quickly understand my situation.

'Where's your office?' I asked.

'Covent Garden.'

'Whereabouts?'

It was right round the corner from my flat, so when I next was in London I went to see her. She was great; she sat me down, explained my options and asked me what had happened. I started to tell her and suddenly I was crying. I must have cried for about an hour; I just couldn't stop. But by the end of the meeting, I knew I had the right person in my corner.

From Joanne's initial text to receiving my Decree Absolute, the whole process took 20 months. That was 20 months of watching my bank account be depleted by one lawyer's invoice after another. Plus the accountants' fees, and all the other professional services and transaction costs. If I could bear to add it all up, then it would come to millions.

Yet it seemed every time I went home, I would turn on the TV and see a story on the news about people losing their jobs, or their benefits, and even though my own bank balance was heading steeply into the red, I knew there were thousands of people who would gladly swap their problems for mine. The money I spent on the divorce could have built several schools in Haiti, or it could have been used to protect dozens of jobs in the UK. Throughout the whole process I just kept thinking 'It doesn't have to be like this'.

When the settlement was finally agreed, we also agreed a confidentiality clause preventing either party from disclosing the details of the divorce. Although it's frustrating that there are things I cannot say, it's probably a good thing as it means we both have to draw a line under what happened and just get on with our lives.

The court accepted that as my wealth is tied up in the business, I couldn't find all the cash straight away. I discussed my options at length with Chris Watson, my finance director, and Nigel Armstrong, my chief executive. We were looking for options that didn't put any additional stress on the company's finances, as we simply could not risk leaving ourselves in breach of the bank's covenants. There weren't any easy solutions, but to preserve the security of the business I had to make some difficult and painful choices that included selling my beloved villa in France.

It was such a bruising experience that I really feel that pre-nups should be as much a part of the wedding planning as hiring the venue or choosing the flowers. And I don't just mean for wealthy people. Talking about money shouldn't be a taboo. Now that people tend to marry later, couples often have very different financial statuses when they tie the knot. If one owns a property when they get married, is it right that it should be divided between them if they divorce a year or two later? And with more and more couples relying on big cash gifts from their parents to get them on the property ladder, isn't it right that their parents' money is protected by a pre-nup? I haven't ruled out marrying for a third time, but there's no way I'd do it without the legal protections of a pre-nup – I owe it to my kids. The only people that lose out from a pre-nup are the divorce lawyers since there will be no argument if things go wrong about who gets what.

I recently had dinner with a friend of mine and his girlfriend. He was widowed a few years ago and has two grown up kids, but is now thinking about getting married for a second time. He would like to get a pre-nup; his girlfriend thinks it is unromantic.

'Personally,' I said, 'I think it's very romantic that he wants to protect his kids. Isn't that one of the things you love about him? Don't you want him to do the right thing?'

She agreed with me, but they still haven't set a date.

Once everything had been finalised, I realised it was time to start rebuilding my life. Time I would have previously spent with Joanne, I now spent with friends and family and it became really important to me to have a base away from anything associated with the divorce where I could relax and enjoy their company.

I would have liked to have bought another villa in France, but I had been spending a lot of time in the Lake District in a cottage owned by my first wife Gail. Tom and I had several weekends away hiring boats and generally mucking about. While we were there, I saw that there were several lakeside lodges for sale at the same holiday park where Gail and I had bought a static caravan nearly thirty years before. I asked him if he'd prefer me to buy another place in France or one of the new lodges on the Fallbarrow site. He was adamant: the lodge.

There's so much for him to do there and he has made so many friends that it is now the place where we spend most of our time together. And when I'm not there, Abigail and Anthony use it, as do my other children. It's certainly not as glamorous as having a villa in the south of France, but I love the fact that the place where we spent so many holidays when they were little still means so much to them now. And hopefully, in years to come, my grandchildren will feel the same way I do about the place.

While I'm thrilled the family gets so much use out of the lodge, I still plan to buy another home abroad just as soon as things calm down a bit on the business front. Spending more time somewhere with better weather than the north of England is very appealing, but I'm keeping an open mind about whether it should be France, or Portugal, or somewhere further afield.

TWENTY-FIVE

Meet the Bandits

There are several people who have really helped me get through the past couple of years. My grown-up daughters have been fantastic (as has my son-in-law Anthony). Nigel and Kim and the rest of the team at the office have been great. The dragons. My friend Noel Edmonds and his wife Liz. My boy Tom. Every one of them has made the lowest points a little easier. But there has also been another group of people in my life who made a huge difference to me while I was going through the divorce. Ben, Andy, Lyndon, Alex and Harry have taught me a great deal, and their company has always made me feel stronger and more positive.

Ben, Andy and Lyndon share something truly remarkable in common: they have all lost limbs. I've already talked about the number of coincidences I've come across during my charity work, and that I should meet all these guys in such a short space of time is another one of those 'coincidences' that feels like something more. I think I am meant to know these men, and my life has been better for it. I've learned so much from each of them.

Ben Parkinson is the most seriously injured soldier to have survived the war in Afghanistan and I met him a year or so before the divorce proceedings started. His armoured vehicle was hit by a roadside bomb and he took the full force of the blast. His injuries were so numerous and so severe that he was immediately airlifted back to the UK so he could die surrounded by his family. Ben had other ideas though, and after a couple of months he emerged from his coma. Although it was clear his life would never be the same again, his friends and family knew that he was still the same old Ben on the inside.

I read about Ben in the papers and got the impression that he lived in Darlington so I got in touch and asked him if he'd like to have lunch with me at the Bannatyne hotel there. It was only when he arrived that I found out he lived in Doncaster and he had made a special trip to meet me. If I had known, I would of course have gone to visit him.

Ben has 56 injuries, the most visible of which is the loss of both legs. He also suffered a stroke. I cannot imagine facing up to the daily challenges he has and yet he is one of the funniest and most positive people I know. At the end of our first lunch together he said something to me. It was a little hard to make out as the stroke has affected his speech.

'Did you just say to me that I have to either give you £5 million or do a parachute jump?' I asked.

'Yeah.' He had this big smile across his face that told me I had just made a new friend.

'You're on.'

A few weeks later, I travelled to an airfield near Southampton where Ben was taking part in a parachute jump. It had been organised by a charity called Pilgrim Bandits that was helping him. There are several charities that help injured service personnel and they all do fantastic work. Pilgrim Bandits has a different ethos because it isn't about raising money for prosthetic limbs or making modifications to soldiers' homes; it does something much simpler – it takes them to the pub. Actually it does more than that. Its mission isn't to get people walking again, it's to get them out from in front of the Xbox and give them the kind of challenges and lifestyle they had before they got injured. Pilgrim Bandits takes them snowboarding, or sailing, or throws them out of an aeroplane.

There were six of us doing a tandem jump that day. We all got strapped to an able-bodied soldier. Ben was the first to leave the plane. I followed. A moment of real terror was immediately replaced with a massive rush of adrenalin: I knew I had to do it again.

I also knew I wanted to support Pilgrim Bandits. So I organised another jump through Twitter. I invited people to come and skydive with us and about 60 people turned up. And as they all had to get £150 in sponsorship on top of their jump fee, it raised quite a bit of money for the charity.

I thought about what else I could do for Ben and some of the other guys I met that day, and hit on the idea of scuba-diving. I mentioned it to Mike, who runs the charity, and he said it was a great idea. The only question was where to do it. I said: 'How about the pool at my villa?'

So Mike, Ben and a couple of other lads flew out to France and we had the most amazing couple of days getting them in the water. For Ben it was a powerful experience because being in the water meant he could move without assistance. It was almost as emotional for those of us watching as it was for him.

It is impossible for me to feel sorry for myself when I'm around Ben, and I really don't think that's because of his injuries – it's because he's just the kind of person who makes you feel good about yourself. I imagine he was just like that before he got injured.

In 2012, I tweeted that all returning soldiers who had lost limbs would automatically get a year's free membership to any Bannatyne health club. Although this was received well by most tweeters, I did get a few haters who sent me a barrage of abuse saying things like 'You will lock them into a contract for two or three years and rip them off', or 'You are only doing this for free publicity'. One of the many people who defended me that day was an amazing guy called Andy Reid who had lost three limbs in Afghanistan.

Andy is incredible. Since getting injured he's become a brilliant motivational speaker and has written a book. He's also got married and had a kid. He's such a positive role model for other people in similar situations that I really wanted him to meet another friend of mine called Lyndon Longhorne.

Lyndon has also lost both legs and an arm, but unlike Andy he can't remember ever being able-bodied. He contracted meningitis as a baby and his limbs were amputated as part of his treatment. The best way I can express Lyndon's amazing character and perseverance is to tell you what his ambition is: to swim at the Paralympics. He narrowly missed out on making the squad in 2012 and has set his sights on making the team for Rio 2016.

I first met Lyndon about eight years ago at an awards ceremony for local heroes in the north-east. He told me he wanted to be a Paralympic swimmer, so I offered him the use of my villa so he could train in the pool. He and his family went out to France a couple of times, and his family and mine became very close – my son Tom really looks up to him.

Getting to know Andy and Ben made me realise that injured soldiers get access to new technology far faster than people like Lyndon. Ben and Andy can both walk on their prosthetic legs, but Lyndon finds his so uncomfortable that he often chooses to use a wheelchair, or to make do without either. Finding a role model when you've lost both your legs and an arm isn't easy, so I really wanted to get Andy and Lyndon together.

And there was someone else I wanted to introduce Lyndon to. At another charity lunch I had met a teenager called Alex Williams. Like Lyndon, he had suffered from meningitis and it left him with many complications and health issues. The poor lad was in constant pain but was determined to raise money for the Meningitis Trust so that other kids wouldn't have to suffer. When I got home, I found him on Twitter and we stayed in touch. Alex was facing the prospect of having a leg amputated, and this was obviously very frightening for him. I thought meeting Lyndon would help take away some of the fear, but I also knew that Lyndon's mum was plugged into a great support network and she would have lots of contacts who could help Alex and his family.

As I've said, it seems more than coincidental to me that in the space of a few years I would meet so many people who had faced up to life after amputation. That feeling increased when I realised that I already knew another person who had faced up to the challenge. My neighbour in London, Matthew, had lost a leg in an accident. He had been asked to take part in the programme *Secret Millionaire*, where rich people go under cover in poor communities to seek out organisations and individuals who could use a bit of help. While filming his episode, Matthew – completely coincidentally – was introduced to Alex.

After filming finished, Matthew helped to pay for modifications to Alex's house so that he could continue to live in his home after his operation. Sadly, this remarkable story has a tragic ending: Alex died in the summer of 2012, just a month after he had been a torch carrier in the Olympic relay.

Alex's funeral hasn't been the only one I have been to in the past few years. In 2010, I went to a charity event with the other dragons and met Harry Moseley, a lovely ten-year-old boy who had a brain tumour. Harry had spent a lot of time in hospital and one of his friends had died: he was selling wristbands to raise money so that other kids wouldn't have to die. He was trying to get as many celebrities to buy them as possible to raise the profile of his campaign. Harry was so enthusiastic that you couldn't be sad around him and we became friends on Twitter. He came along to the parachute jump, where he sold more of his bracelets, and it was just great to see him brighten up so many people's days.

In 2011, Harry became ill again and he was taken into hospital, where he was in a coma. When I went to visit him, I sat and chatted to him and I felt his hand pressing down on mine: his mum, Georgie, was sure that he knew it was me.

Georgie was amazing. She stayed with Harry the entire time he was in hospital; the only time she left his bedside was to get changed in the toilets. While I was there, the doctors said they had some test results and asked if Georgie wanted to wait for Harry's dad to arrive before they discussed them. She said she wanted to know straight away, so I was with her when they told her there was nothing more they could do for Harry. In seven days, they said, they would have to switch off his life support. It was an absolutely devastating situation but Georgie handled it with such strength and grace. She asked if she could take Harry home to die, which is what happened.

A few weeks later, I found myself in the Moseleys' kitchen with Ben Shepherd from GMTV who had also come to pay his respects. It was an extraordinary and very moving funeral. Harry had touched so many people's lives and there were hundreds of people lining the streets. I'll never forget that day, and I'll never forget Harry: I have several photos of him in my office.

In early 2013, I decided it was time to finally get Andy and Lyndon together. Since Lyndon has become very good friends with my son Tom, I invited him to come and stay with us in the Lake District. I had recently bought the lodge there and Tom and I were enjoying weekends out on the water on my new speedboat: I thought Lyndon would enjoy it too. I also got in touch with Andy and asked him if he would be able to come to visit while Lyndon was with us.

One of the main reasons I wanted to get the two of them together was because, at the age of 17, Lyndon was still having trouble with his prosthetic limbs and was mostly using his wheelchair (or just bouncing along the ground on his bottom, something he is very good at – and *very* fast). Absolutely nothing holds him back – he can bounce up flights of stairs and along jetties onto my boat – but he very seldom puts his legs on simply because he has to use them with crutches and he is more agile without them. However, I knew that Andy was doing much better on his prosthetic legs because ex-service personnel have access to the best facilities, and I wondered if he could help.

Although Andy and I had been in touch on Twitter for a year or so, we had never actually met. The first time I saw him was in the pub at the Fallbarrow lodge site and it was such an honour to finally shake his hand. Losing both legs and an arm hasn't held him back, and seeing him in the pub with his wife Clare and their new baby William was inspirational for all of us, not just Lyndon.

Andy was astonished at the old-fashioned prosthetic limbs Lyndon was using and the lack of assistance he was getting. Andy told us about his doctor at the Preston Limb Centre and said he would put the two of them in touch. You could see from Lyndon's face that things he had previously thought impossible were becoming possible: he wanted to see how Andy managed to drive his car, and he wanted to learn how he had managed to become completely independent. Listening to them was amazing: even though they had similar disabilities, they had such different experiences, starting with the fact that Andy had grown up with four limbs but Lyndon had never known what that was like.

That night, a group of 20 of us went for dinner in a restaurant in Bowness. As well as Andy, Clare and William, we were joined by Lyndon's parents, my daughter Abigail and her family, and my first wife Gail and her boyfriend. It was going to be a long and noisy night.

When we were getting ready, Lyndon told me and Tom that he wanted to put his legs on to go to the restaurant. I am pretty sure it was the inspiration he had already gained from meeting Andy that made him decide he was going to walk – and walk he did.

The last time I had been to a restaurant with Lyndon wearing his legs he had taken them off during the meal because they were so uncomfortable, but this time he kept them on and afterwards he walked the mile back to the lodge. Tom made me very proud by offering to push Lyndon's chair the whole way in case he found it too much. The two of them set off together (Tom chose to wheel himself in the chair rather than walk!) while the rest of us stayed for another drink. When I got back to the lodge, the lads told me that Lyndon hadn't needed his chair: he'd walked the whole way there and he'd been determined to walk the whole way back too.

The next day I took Lyndon, Andy, Clare and a few others out for a spin in the boat. I always insist all passengers wear a life jacket and always have enough of them in the boat for guests. Tom and I handed them round, but when I checked everyone was ready to go, I noticed Andy had buckled his jacket but hadn't zipped it up.

'You need to do your jacket up, mate,' I told him.

He gave me a quizzical look.

'It needs zipping,' I said.

Then it hit me, the way a punch hits you when you let your guard down in the boxing ring: he couldn't zip up his jacket because he only has one hand. I couldn't believe what an idiot I was. My only defence is that because Andy is so independent it just didn't occur to me that he needed help. He completely embodies the motto of Pilgrim Bandits: no sympathy.

I stepped over and zipped it up for him while trying to hide my embarrassment and then we set off. I let Tom drive for a bit and he showed off his skills doing some James Bond turns, making us all thankful we were wearing those life jackets!

The following day, I got a text from Andy: 'Hi mate, just been to Preston Limb Centre and spoke to Dr Jepson. Said he will get in touch with Lyndon and get him over for a consultation soon.'

My eyes filled with tears of happiness. I texted back: 'FANTASTIC. I think I love you.'

Like I say, Andy Reid is a truly inspirational guy and I can't wait for the day when Lyndon is walking without the aid of crutches.

TWENTY-SIX

Reaching the Top

When I landed after jumping out of a plane for the second time to raise money for Pilgrim Bandits, Ben Parkinson said he thought I needed a new challenge. The charity was in the process of organising a fund-raising expedition to Mount Kilimanjaro and he thought I should join the team.

Kilimanjaro is the highest mountain in Africa. It's a popular destination for tourists and fund-raising groups – Comic Relief sent a bunch of celebrities a few years ago – as it is possible to reach the summit without climbing gear. It's more like trekking than mountain-climbing and so doesn't require any special training. That doesn't mean it's easy. Far from it. Many people don't make it to the top, and a few never make it back down to the bottom. But when someone challenges me to do something, there's a part of me that just has to prove I can do it. I said yes.

I started doing some research on how to prepare for the climb, and realised that most of the people in the photos at the summit were a lot younger than me. I was approaching my 63rd birthday. Although there is no upper age limit to taking on the challenge – a few people in their eighties have managed it – I knew I was going to find it tough.

I'm in pretty good shape for my age (after all, I do own the best chain of health clubs in the country!), but I knew it was going to be hard going. I made some changes to my workout and diet in an attempt to get ready. Tom and I went out walking in the hills around the Lakes, but when we got home and googled the peaks we had climbed, I found out they were only about a tenth of the height of Kilimanjaro. And I hadn't been carrying a rucksack.

When I mentioned it to Hollie, she said she wanted to come with me. I think she wanted to keep an eye on me, but she also wanted to support Ben and the other Pilgrim Bandits. And she likes a challenge too.

'You do realise it means sharing a tent?' I asked her.

'With you?'

'Yes.'

'Well I guess that's better than sharing with a stranger.'

I knew I would be away for a couple of weeks so I wanted to spend as much time as possible with Tom and Emily before I left. I was making them dinner at my new house – cooking is something I've started to do a lot of since the divorce – when Emily said something that turned out to be very significant.

'You know Dad, Mum doubts you'll make it to the top of Kilimanjaro.'

That had just given me even more motivation to make it. So a few days after my 63rd birthday, Hollie and I got on a plane to Tanzania and arranged to meet up with the Pilgrim Bandits party.

There were about 25 of us, including four injured soldiers who had each lost a leg. One of them, John, worked for Pilgrim Bandits, and during the climb I found out how he'd lost his leg – in a speedboating accident. I had assumed all the soldiers' injuries had come from the battlefield, but Kilimanjaro quickly teaches you to ditch your preconceptions. Although we were a very mixed group, we always had something to talk about – whether chatting about the view or a piece of kit or asking for a blister plaster, there is something very bonding about sharing an experience like this with total strangers. The fact that some of them recognised me from TV stopped mattering after we'd climbed a few feet; it just wasn't an issue.

The determination of those four injured soldiers gave the rest of us strength. Whenever it got tough on the climb, we always knew it was tougher for them, and yet they pushed on. Apart from John, they each had an able-bodied soldier trekking with them to give them support when they needed it, but that in no way lessened the challenge it was for them. One soldier, Ricky, had lost his leg 18 months previously and had only had his new leg for 6 months: a lot of the group thought it was too big a challenge for someone in his position, but he was absolutely determined to prove them wrong.

The other people in the group were supporters of the charity, all of whom were being sponsored to get to the top. I had collected about £4,000 in pledges: knowing what £4,000 means to an organisation like Pilgrim Bandits was a huge incentive to make sure I made it to the summit.

There are guides who carry your tent for you, but we had to carry our own clothes, water and food. Although it's quite a gentle slope to begin with, you can't walk up Kilimanjaro in a straight line, since doing that doesn't give you time to acclimatise to the altitude. Instead you have to make the ascent in a zigzag. We set off in incredible heat through tropical rainforest, surrounded by trees and greenery and the non-stop sounds of birds and frogs. It seemed incredible that we were climbing a mountain.

On the second day we walked through a completely different landscape of shale and could see the rainforest below us. It was tempting to go faster, but the guides kept reminding us to slow down – we had to give our bodies a chance to get used to the reduced oxygen.

For the first couple of days there is still quite a lot of oxygen in the air. Your feet aren't yet *completely* covered in blisters, and you start to think 'This isn't so bad, I'll definitely be able to make it.' But by the end of day three you are beginning to realise how far away the summit is.

As the air gets thinner, everything becomes harder. You feel yourself slowing down, yet you want to make progress. You really want to make it to that night's camp so you can collapse, but whenever I started to pick up speed, the guides would say to me 'poleypoley' which is the Swahili for 'slowly'. Poleypoley, poleypoley: after a few days, the words got permanently lodged in my brain.

On day three, we had several steep climbs and it was important for us to pace ourselves: the paths were narrow and if we slipped we could get badly hurt. Hollie was walking ahead of me and at one point she completely froze. When I got closer to her I realised why: she was standing at the edge of a sheer drop. Although there were plenty of ropes to hold on to, she just couldn't move. She was having a panic attack in the worst possible place.

One of the guides was just above her on the climb, and I was just below her. We could see where she needed to move her arms and her feet, but she was too petrified to move.

The guide took hold of her arms and I held one of her feet.

'Trust me,' I said, as calmly as I could. 'Hollie, hold on with both hands, don't move your left foot but release your right foot and let me move it.' I moved her foot and made sure it was firmly in the hole then said, 'Now hold on with both hands while I move your left foot.'

The guide then moved her hands and I moved her feet again. We did this until the path widened out and Hollie was able to move herself. She was completely fine afterwards, but it was a real lesson on how vulnerable you are in places like that – none of us know how we're going to react in unfamiliar situations. I have never been afraid of heights but that does not make me brave: bravery is overcoming your fears as Hollie did. I guess the big question now is if I will ever get her to skydive! It takes seven days of slowly zigzagging upwards to reach the summit. By day four I was seriously beginning to wonder if I could make it. I was definitely getting weaker and my guide would no longer let me carry my own rucksack. My thoughts were so full of putting one foot in front of the other that entire hours went by when I forgot about all my other problems. My phone still worked, and I still got messages and tweets that encouraged me to carry on, but I found the climb so demanding that it pushed out all other thoughts. It was very hard on my body, but at the same time it gave my brain a much needed holiday from the divorce.

On the fifth day, Hollie fell ill – apparently, fit young people are more likely to get altitude sickness. She just had to lie down in our tent. I brought her food, but she could barely move. I went to talk to the soldiers who were also finding the last few days incredibly hard going. One of the injured guys didn't think he could make it – the headaches from the altitude sickness were just so bad.

When I was getting some food, I noticed one of the able-bodied soldiers was practically in the fetal position, rocking with the pain. He looked terrible, but he said he would not let his partner down. He had to help him get to the top, no matter how bad he felt himself. Those guys were incredible. Not only were they doing everything the rest of us were doing, but they were also carrying their partner's gear and doing it without complaining. I really felt for this guy; he was in agony but he wasn't giving up.

The closer we got to the top, the harder it got. One of the injured guys decided he wasn't going to make it, and reluctantly he and his climbing partner turned back. It was incredibly hard to see them walk off in the opposite direction: they had already achieved so much and you could see the pain of making the decision on their faces. Having come so far, they wanted so much to reach the top, but the soldier having trouble felt he was putting the rest of us at risk.

Hollie started to feel better just as I started to feel sick.

It wasn't altitude sickness, it was a stomach bug. We had been snacking on things like popcorn in the evenings, and I guess maybe someone in the group hadn't washed their hands properly. Having diarrhoea is horrible when you're at home; having it at 16,000ft when you're using an outside toilet and the temperature is close to freezing makes it much, much worse. On the fifth night, I had to go to the toilet 14 times. I barely slept. I couldn't eat. I felt so, so weak. But it was the day we were due to reach high camp: I had to carry on.

We only had to walk four or five hours that day as you reach the final camp at lunchtime. You then sleep until 11pm and leave for the summit in darkness so that you get to the top in time to see the sun rise over the African plain. It's the prospect of that once-in-a-lifetime sight that's supposed to motivate you to keep putting one foot in front of the other. Unless you happen to feel as ill as I did, that is. I was physically exhausted. I had had the worst diarrhoea I could ever remember. I hadn't eaten. I didn't have enough oxygen in my blood. I felt so fucking terrible. And yet I couldn't sleep.

Hollie and I spoke to our guide and asked if we could start our climb early. There seemed little point in waiting for an hour because if we left there and then, we would have an extra hour for the walk and I really felt like I needed to take it slowly. The guide agreed, and the three of us formed an advance party and headed for the top.

We were so high up that it was well below freezing. We had set off in tropical heat but now I was wearing six layers of clothing, which made walking even harder. Poleypoley,

poleypoley. At one point I just had to stop; I couldn't manage another step. The rest of the group caught up and passed us. When I eventually felt like I could carry on, Hollie and I started walking again. We caught up with some of our group – one of the injured guys had had to stop because his leg was causing him so much pain. Normally we would have sat with him and encouraged him, but it took everything I had just to stay awake.

'I'm really sorry, I can't stop. If I sit down I'll never get back up.'

They all understood. We were all feeling it.

Hollie and I kept plodding along. Every step hurt. It was three in the morning. It was dark. It was minus 15 degrees and I suddenly reached my limit. There was nothing left. I fell over face down in the snow. I don't know how long I was there for but I was aware of one of the guides talking to me.

'Get up,' he was saying, 'you'll die if you don't.'

He started kicking me to get me to move but I couldn't. 'People die up here,' he said. 'Come on, you've got to get up.'

I wasn't cold, I wasn't in pain, and I just wanted to lie there. Was I asleep? Then Hollie came up to me.

'Dad, listen to me. You need to get up. GET UP!' My daughter's voice reached a part of my brain that the guide's hadn't.

'I can't go any further.'

'But you have to, Dad, you have to.'

'Why?'

'You know why!'

She helped me to my feet and we started walking again.

After another hour or so we saw something that looked as if it might be the summit – there was a hut on the spot. But when we made it to that hut at about six in the morning we realised it was just a staging post. We were close, yet our goal had never felt further away. I was fading fast. I just wanted to lie down. I just wanted to close my eyes.

I remember looking at the track in front of me thinking that it was ten footsteps before we had to turn. 'I can do that in my sleep,' I thought. And so I closed my eyes and kept walking. After three or four steps I stumbled and I was back on the ground, sound asleep. It happened three or four times. I was awake, and then a second later I was so deeply asleep that I was having vivid dreams.

Somehow, I made it to the summit. I was too exhausted to be elated. I took my BlackBerry out to take a photo, but it had frozen. The guide came over and took a picture of Hollie and me and after that I just wanted – needed – to go back down.

'But the sun will come up in half an hour. You'll miss it.'

I didn't care, I just had to get to my bed. Hollie and I started our descent. I fell again and was asleep before I hit the ground. I had this most beautiful, fantastic dream that I was in a warm place. I felt peaceful, but then I was aware of a woman's voice. She seemed irritated, but all I wanted to do was sleep. I just wanted to stay there. Forever. 'If I die here,' I thought, 'that's OK.' Then someone kicked me and I was awake again. I could still hear the woman's voice behind me, talking in a foreign language and realised it was one of the other people in our party. I was so disorientated I felt like I had been drugged. But I had no option but to get up once more and continue to walk slowly down the mountain. Somehow I made it back to the tent.

It was an enormous physical and mental achievement for me to make it to the summit, but I was even more thrilled for the Bandits who made it, particularly Ricky. His determination, his will-power, had been so great that even though he was obviously in a lot of pain for much of the climb, there was just no stopping him.

It takes two days to walk back down the mountain, and when we made camp at the end of that day we discovered that three people had died in other groups on Kilimanjaro during the night. I think I came close to joining them. The people who died were an 83-year-old woman who fell and hit her head; an experienced guide who had a heart attack; and a young man with water on his lungs who had been brought up to our camp from a lower group because we had a doctor in our party. Our doctor had to tell the guides that the thing the patient needed was to go down the mountain, not up. By trying to get him quick medical attention they had probably caused his death. She was devastated that she hadn't been able to help.

On the second day of our descent, Hollie marched in front of me; she couldn't stop. Even though I was still wearing all my layers, I didn't seem to have the energy to take them off: all I could do was walk. It got hotter and hotter as we got down, and I could feel the sweat clinging to my clothes. I had even slept in my boots as I was just too exhausted to take them off. No wonder that when I finally got in the shower back at the hotel and looked down at my feet, the water was black. Filthy.

Unsurprisingly, I slept well that night. I felt very proud of myself for not giving up but even more proud of my wonderful daughter. In the morning, we flew back to the UK. And back to the recession.

TWENTY-SEVEN

Business as Usual?

At some point in 2010, back in the days when I thought I was still happily married, Bannatyne Fitness was approached by an agent with a couple of clubs to sell who wanted to know if we were interested in buying them. We asked for some background information and were told that the clubs had been built by a housing developer – often to get planning permission for new developments you have to include some commercial facilities. When the housing market started to decline this property developer realised he needed to liquidise a few of his assets.

I grew Bannatyne Fitness by building health clubs from scratch – buying the land, getting permission and sending the builders in. But in the past seven or eight years, there just haven't been that many opportunities to build new clubs. This is partly because land values rose significantly before the recession, due to the residential housing boom, but also because the market is quite mature now, and most locations that can sustain a health club already have one. That means the most likely source of growth for Bannatyne Fitness will be through acquisition. Following the successful integration of the LivingWell clubs into the Bannatyne Group, this is something we've become quite good at. We know that we can often turn a profit in locations where other operators have struggled because we have such good management structures, with the added benefit of centralised payroll, invoicing and customer service from our HQ in Darlington.

The two clubs – one in Manchester and one in Bedfordshire – were an interesting proposition for us, so we looked into them carefully. One club was freehold, the other leasehold. The freehold club was making in the region of £560,000 annual profit but the leasehold one was losing money, and as a business is valued as a multiple of profit, we had to value the leasehold club at zero.

The freehold club had a spa area that was only half fitted out; we knew that we could complete the spa and start to make increased profits from it so we offered £4.75 million for both clubs. We thought the acquisition was a pretty good fit for us, but we had two problems: firstly we didn't have the money to buy the clubs and secondly we couldn't borrow the money to buy them.

We had meetings with lots of banks and brokers, but no one was prepared to lend money to Bannatyne Fitness because IBRC already had the first charge over our assets and it wasn't possible to ring-fence any new debt inside the company.

Back in 2010, I still had some money in the bank. It wasn't enough to buy the clubs outright, but it was enough to use as a deposit if we could ever find a bank to lend us the balance. However, I was reluctant to put this cash into the business because if the next valuation found us in breach, Anglo Irish could simply keep that money.

So I had an idea. Having separate companies had allowed me to borrow more when we were expanding rapidly in the early days of the business. I thought the time was right to start Bannatyne Fitness 2 for the second time. Putting my spare cash into a new company meant the gearing levels in Bannatyne Fitness 1 were irrelevant. We were reducing the risk for a new lender and making it a simpler proposition for them. Even so, when we went back to the brokers and lenders with Bannatyne Fitness 2, we still found that most of them were in no mood to lend. However, one bank was happy to make us an offer.

Handelsbanken is a Swedish bank, and although it's been operating in the UK since the 1980s I had never heard of it. Its business model was a bit different from that of the better-known banks – all it did was take money in from savers and pay them interest, then lend that money out to borrowers at a slightly higher rate. While practically every other bank in the world was turning itself into a casino, Handelsbanken was still behaving like a bank from the 1970s. And in 2011, that meant it still had some money to lend out. So we borrowed the money and added two new clubs to our business, one of which we had effectively bought for nothing.

The leasehold club only had eight months left to run on its lease and we had to give the freeholder six months' notice if we didn't intend to renew it. So two months after the purchase, we gave notice on the lease. The freeholder got in touch.

'Why aren't you renewing?'

'The club is losing money after paying the rent.'

Knowing that he would find it very difficult to find another tenant, he asked if there was anything he could do.

'You could reduce the rent by half.'

Facing the prospect of our suggestion or no income at all and an empty property slowly becoming derelict, the landlord agreed to halve the rent. This meant the club became profitable, so we've kept it open and everyone is happy. It doesn't make a lot of money, but as it didn't cost us anything to buy, that is OK by us.

As soon as we got the keys of the other club, our team moved in and overhauled it. First of all we completed the spa facilities and got them operational, but we also restructured the organisation to make it more efficient. The support and guidance we can give to club managers and their teams means we can create a better environment and offer better services than any independent operator. And because we have centralised a lot of the back-office expenditure, we can make even more profit. Within a few months, we had increased the profits by £80,000 a year. As an organisation, and as a team, this is something we're very good at, and I'm incredibly proud of the guys who go into a new club and make a success of it so quickly.

For me, this shows that no matter how bad the financial picture, there are always opportunities. It's very easy when things are tough to batten down the hatches and shut yourself off: you spend so much of your time just trying to survive that you don't look towards the future. But a business that doesn't look to grow and doesn't take those chances to expand will inevitably be overtaken by a younger, hungrier rival at some point.

Being flexible is as important in a big company as it is in a start-up. I sometimes wonder if the companies that don't make it through tough economic times are not the ones with poor balance sheets or inferior products but the ones with leaders and managers who are wearing the business equivalent of horse's blinkers. They become so fixed on one thing – in our case it could have been the Anglo Irish situation – that they don't see that other opportunities are there to be explored. I'm proud of the fact that my team and I have retained the hunger to expand, and the flexibility to make things happen when an opportunity presents itself.

Sadly, my divorce has really had an impact on that flexibility. I no longer have any money in the bank because it all went to Joanne or the lawyers. I cannot increase our borrowing levels because at some point soon, I won't just have to pay off Anglo Irish, I will also have to pay Joanne. There really aren't reserves of capital to play with. And when you can't borrow, it's capital that gives you flexibility.

Since 2012, we've had to make twelve people redundant that I'm confident would still have a job if it weren't for the problems around cash flow.

Some of the people we let go were in our developments team, so it was pretty easy to explain to the remaining staff why they were the ones to leave: we're just not taking on enough new developments at the moment. Some of the other redundancies came when we shut down the crèches in a couple of our clubs, and again it was not hard to explain that decision. Not enough people were using the crèches, and we calculated that if we closed them only a handful of members would cancel their agreements with us, and that would cost us a lot less than we were currently paying in salaries to the childminders. When the other staff could see the financial sense in the move – and were reassured that this actually helped to safeguard their own jobs – they were supportive of the changes. Of course, the crèche staff were encouraged to apply for any other vacancies that came up in the business.

I have a great HR manager and we have really good systems within the business to deal with situations like redundancies. We always make sure that staff are treated well and informed not just of the management's decision, but also of the reasons behind that decision. Good communication doesn't cost an organisation very much at all, but non-existent communication can be incredibly expensive in terms of morale. No matter how difficult things get at board level, managers should never forget that everyone else in the business will be facing their own problems.

So far, though, I'm pleased to say that our team seem to be getting through the tough times in relatively good shape. It's been an odd recession in that respect. I remember at the last Christmas party I was speaking to some of our call-centre staff and was expecting to get the usual comments of 'Can I have a pay rise please, Duncan?', but most of the people I spoke to were just so happy to have a job that morale has stayed high.

Many of our call-centre staff are single mums who only work two days a week and get help in the form of tax credits. Everyone's feeling the pinch, but so long as they can keep their two-day-a-week job, they can feel secure about the future. For people who have held on to their jobs, the low interest rates mean that most of them are getting through this recession in a way I don't remember happening in the 1980s. For those with tracker mortgages, it's actually been a very good recession, and as long as interest rates stay low, it looks like we'll all muddle through together.

As I say, it's been an odd recession: our clubs are still full, our hotels get overbooked, our spas are becoming more profitable, and when I walk through London or get a cab through Manchester, I see busy bars and queues outside restaurants. And yet when I get home or back to my hotel room and flick on the TV, the headlines are all doom and gloom.

TWENTY-EIGHT

Entrepreneur Nation

I've often heard it said that a recession is a really good time to start a business. The thinking is that if you can survive in tough times, then you'll thrive when things pick up. The truth is that it's always a good time to start a business.

There's no doubt that shows like *Dragons' Den* and *The Apprentice* – not to mention *Mary Queen of Shops* or *Property Ladder* – have encouraged more and more Britons to start thinking about how they can make money for themselves rather than for their employer. When I first started my ice-cream business, setting up on your own was seen as the risky option. These days, there is an understanding that sometimes the best way to secure a job for yourself is to create one. I can't imagine a father telling a son any more – as my dad did – that 'people like us don't start businesses'. I think parents today are far more likely to see their child setting up for themselves as a good thing and I'm thrilled if that's in part because of the success of people like me. I called my first book *Anyone Can Do It* because I really believe that anyone can do what I have done. For those people made redundant from shrinking industries, or shut out from joining companies that can't afford to expand, I truly believe that setting up on your own is the best route forward.

Thanks to *Dragons' Den*, I regularly meet new entrepreneurs – both inside and outside the Den – and I know that it's no longer possible to start a business the way I did. We no longer get the offers through our doors for unsecured 'any purpose loans', and there are no more ads on TV encouraging equity release from our properties. Getting into debt is no longer the quickest way of getting into business, but if there is some good news to come out of the recession it's that it has created lots of low-cost ways to start a business. Times are different now, but they're not necessarily tougher if you spot the right opportunity.

Commercial landlords all over the country are suffering when their tenants go bust – that's why the landlord of one of our clubs slashed the rent when we asked him to. In the past, empty retail premises became charity shops, but now the trend is for 'pop-up' shops. These are run by creative entrepreneurs (often young) who take over a shop – sometimes for a reduced rent, occasionally free – and start selling their wares. They don't bother refitting the premises as they don't know how long they will be allowed to operate for (usually the pay-off for cheap rent is a very short notice period), but this saves massively on start-up costs and lets entrepreneurs put their products in front of consumers very easily.

It's not just shops: pop-up restaurants have become a

big new trend all over the world, and finding the newest, oddest place for a meal has become something to brag about everywhere from Manchester to New York to Cape Town. There's also been a big trend towards food trucks, which allow new chefs and entrepreneurs to learn their trade without the expense of renting and maintaining premises.

Wherever I look, I see young entrepreneurs finding low-cost ways to start a business, and who knows if the dress designer in a pop-up shop is going to be the next Stella McCartney, or if the guy flipping gourmet burgers in his food van is the next Gordon Ramsay. Perhaps, like me in my ice-cream days, he'll end up with a fleet of vans and he'll find a way to make a fortune.

What I find really encouraging about the pop-up trend is that it gives people a relatively risk-free experience of running a business. Some of them will find they are good at it, and may go on to run a bigger business one day, but even those who don't will gain skills that will be useful no matter what direction their career takes.

Of course, the really big difference between now and when I bought my ice-cream van isn't the lending climate, it's the internet. In my view, it has never been easier to start a business because the internet makes everything so much quicker and cheaper. Instead of needing a physical shop, you can buy a website domain name and be up and running in a few hours. Or you can sell products on eBay, Etsy or Amazon's Marketplace.

You can download business-plan templates, you can reach out to customers through Twitter and Facebook, and you can maintain relationships with clients in forums and online networking groups. You can also get support from other entrepreneurs, while innovations like Google Ads mean you can pay to reach only those customers that are searching for your product or service – far more cost-effective than traditional advertising in magazines or on the radio. Starting a business online can be unbelievably quick and cheap, and it's something anyone can do from their kitchen table.

I don't know what the average age of a first-time entrepreneur is, but I'm willing to bet that it's a lot younger than it used to be. The low entry cost of starting a business online means that it's a route more and more people are taking, even teenagers who've never had a pay packet before. It helps that there are now lots of role models for young entrepreneurs, from Fraser Doherty, the Scottish teenager who started SuperJam, to Londoner Nick D'Aloisio who sold his Summly app to Yahoo for millions in 2013. There's no doubt that Nick's success, and the success of companies like Tumblr, which sold to Yahoo for over $1 billion, will encourage even more teenage entrepreneurs to have a go. I just hope they realise it doesn't matter if they don't emulate that level of success: what matters is that they learn the basics of business, and gain the skills and confidence to start another business, and then another.

Of course, the problem with internet businesses is that there are so many of them it is very difficult to get noticed. For every Summly, there are hundreds of thousands of apps that are only ever downloaded by a handful of people. Even good apps, and good online businesses, will fail if their founders don't employ old-fashioned marketing skills to reach potential customers. It isn't enough to build a brilliant website, or create an amazing app: you still need to tell people about it. The fundamentals of running a successful business haven't changed.

However, I have a theory that because it can take so little of an entrepreneur's time and money to build an online business, that makes it easier for them to walk away from it. If you have spent £450 of your hard-earned money on an ice-cream van and it's parked outside your front door, I think you're much more motivated to go out and sell your product than if you've spent a fiver and five minutes at your computer. The dragons are always looking for evidence that entrepreneurs are fully invested – financially and emotionally – in their businesses, and this is because the more committed people are, the more likely it is that they will fight to make their business a success.

Franchise businesses have also been very successful recently, again because they are a low-risk way to get started. Many of the people who have bought franchises for the stage-school company Razzamataz in the past few years have just been made redundant and are using their pay-offs to set themselves up for the future. Buying a franchise is perfect for a lot of people who either don't have an idea for their own business, or need a bit of support. Razzamataz – one of my most successful Den investments – offers a low-cost way of starting your own business and gives franchisees lots of advice to ensure they are successful. Denise Hutton-Gosney, who founded the business, tells me that the franchise fairs she visits have never been busier.

For my generation, there was the prospect of a job for life if you joined the right firm and didn't rock the boat, but in the past few decades, job security has become a rarity. Instead of getting to the end of their career with one or two employers on their CV, today's workers might have 20 or even 30. Plenty of people who have a job often have a second career or do a bit of freelancing on the side, but the great thing about the internet is that your second job can easily be your first business. If you're buying and selling on eBay, or designing apps, a few hours a night after you get home from work could be all you need to start securing a bright future for yourself.

TWENTY-NINE

Good Management

Although it's my name above the door, the truth is that if I took a year off the business probably wouldn't suffer at all. The most important person working for the company these days is Nigel Armstrong, my chief executive.

My role within the company is now to support Nigel and the rest of the board. We aim to have board meetings every three months: the board members – aside from Nigel and myself – are Chris Watson, the finance director, Steve Hancock, who oversees the maintenance of our clubs and hotels, and Justin Musgrove, who was promoted to commercial director after doing such a good job on the spa side of the business. Justin now also looks after our voucher sales and our website and is looking to get our spa products into retailers.

Although I will usually see one of them whenever I am in the office, the fact is that with so many properties it's pretty rare for all five of us to be in the office at the same time, which is why it's important that we make a formal appointment to meet once a quarter. In the week before the board meeting, we will all put whatever we want on the agenda, and on the day of the meeting we don't leave the room until we've reached agreement on each item. It usually takes around three hours, but during the divorce and some of the more difficult bank negotiations, there was enough on the agenda for the meeting to take all day.

It's very important that we all know what the others have planned. It's also important that when we agree on something at a board meeting, it is implemented as agreed. The great thing about the Bannatyne Group is that because the board is so small, and because we all trust each other to do our jobs, everything is straightforward: a decision gets made and the change gets implemented. I never feel the need to chase up any of the board members to get a progress report because I know they'll just be getting on with whatever we agreed.

It's so different from when I ran Quality Care Homes after it became a public company. The City insisted we had two non-executive directors, whom I only ever saw at board meetings and whose only concern was the share price. As the biggest shareholder in the company, I think I was the person with the greatest interest in the share price, but there were many times when I wanted to do something and they advised against it. They measured the company's success solely by the share price, but I always thought that was the wrong measure as it can so easily be manipulated: profit is ultimately the best measure of a company's success. The rows we had were immense, which is why I appreciate the way we run things now. It's so much simpler, so much more efficient (and, of course, we don't have to pay inflated salaries to non-execs who don't contribute anything).

If I'm in the country, I will usually be in the office most weeks, unless I'm filming. It would be very easy for me to pop my head round every door and 'just catch up' with different managers, but that would be absolutely the wrong thing to do. For starters it would take them away from the work they are doing, but it would also interfere with the chain of command – they report to Nigel, not me.

The idea that they need to run things past me is actually quite funny as their sector expertise and their hands-on experience means that a lot of the time it should probably be me running things past them! If I am asked to sit in on an interview for a senior appointment I'm happy to do so, but if I'm not available, I completely trust my HR director and Nigel to choose the best candidate. I am very clear that they can't defer to me or second-guess what I would do – I employ them because they are better at their jobs than I would be.

Delegation is something I have always been comfortable with, although I know that many people have trouble with it. A lot of entrepreneurs seem to be control freaks and either don't trust anyone else to do as good as job as they do, or simply can't let go. By contrast, there are also those who are too keen to let someone else do the jobs they don't enjoy. That's almost as bad: the first jobs to delegate should be those which can be most effectively carried out by someone else, not the ones you don't like. A good example of a job worth delegating is getting an accountant to do your tax return – they're probably better and quicker at it than you would be.

The fact that this also happens to be a job most people don't like doing is just a bonus!

Once you've identified the best jobs to hand over to someone else, the secret of effective delegation is incredibly simple: firstly, agree a brief and set out exactly what you want done; secondly, agree a budget and a timescale for the work; and thirdly, leave them to get on with it. It's usually the last point that most new entrepreneurs have difficulty with, as often they have fixed ideas about how things should be done. What they don't realise is that it doesn't matter *how* a job is done, only that's it's done on time, on budget and to the required standard. The details should no longer be your concern – the whole point of delegation is to free you up to think strategically and grow the business.

These days, my role within the company is also to be a bit of a figurehead. We've done research and we know that we get more enquiries about memberships when I appear on TV, and when I go on the radio to promote a book or a charity event, it also benefits the company. When I travel round the country, I will always visit the clubs we have in the area and when I stay at the lodge in the Lake District, I'll request a session with a personal trainer from our club in Carlisle. I'll do the same when I stay at our hotels or spend time in London – it's a really simple way of staying connected to our staff and it allows me to monitor our standards around the country.

I have always had a poster in every club and every hotel with my email address on it. I want staff and members to know that I care about what happens in the clubs. They tell me that knowing that they can always contact me if they have concerns is reassuring. I don't get many emails, which I take as a good sign that everyone's happy, but when I do, I still get on the case and make sure their problems are sorted out.

Day-to-day I don't think there's anything I do when I'm in the office that wouldn't get done if I wasn't there. Nigel could handle the lot – he and I have worked together for so long that we know how each other thinks. But he is also very busy, so there is no harm in sharing the load a bit. One of the ways I can still make a difference is by being a sounding board for him; sometimes it helps to have another brain consider a problem.

One of the important things I do when I'm in the office is scrutinise our monthly figures. We produce monthly profit and loss accounts for each club and for each income stream within the clubs – whether that's personal training, the café, merchandise or the vending machines. I go through the figures looking for any club that's performing above or below the average. If one club has worked out a way of selling a lot more merchandise, then we need to learn what they've been doing and roll it out to all our clubs.

I recently noticed one of our café bars was taking less than clubs of a comparable size, so I asked for a breakdown of exactly what they were selling, and – crucially – what percentage of their income was in cash. It's sad to say, but where there's cash there is also temptation, and the cost to a business of handling cash seems to get higher every year. I like the fact that the vast majority of our income – from memberships, hotel stays, spa treatments and dinners in our hotels – is paid by credit or debit card. The cost of processing payments is much less than the 'slippage' we experience when bills are settled in cash. It was by comparing the average across the group that we uncovered two clubs with areas which were underperforming significantly. When we investigated why, we found out that members were paying for some services in cash.

Sometimes, the reason why one club – or one area of a club – is doing better or worse than another won't be obvious. Even if you ask the staff involved they often won't know. This is when I find mystery shoppers are very useful. All our staff know we use them and there is always a chance that the customer they are serving is going to report back to Nigel and me. It's a great way for us to find out what is really going on: a lot of the time they use cameras and we can actually see how members of staff behave or how clean the clubs really are. For us, it's a highly cost-effective management tool.

And, of course, we don't just use them on our premises. The only way to really find out what our rivals are offering is to send in our own spies. Sometimes this will be family and friends, but the benefit of using mystery shoppers is that they are brilliant negotiators. They will haggle with a rival operator so skilfully that we can be sure what their lowest possible price is.

Although the Bannatyne Group is made up of four separate companies – Bannatyne Fitness 1 and 2, Bannatyne Hotels and Bannatyne Properties – the business effectively operates as one company. It makes no sense to have separate back-end services, so things like payroll, legal matters and HR are all handled by Bannatyne Fitness, which in turn pays rent to Bannatyne Properties for the HQ. We have the same person negotiating with the breweries to supply the hotels and the clubs, as well as the Bannatyne bar in Newcastle, as it wouldn't make sense to have four separate negotiations.

It does not only make financial sense to operate as one company: there are other advantages. Sometimes you learn something from one industry that you can apply to another, and there are also opportunities for our staff to get experience in more than one sector. Recently, for example, the manager of our Darlington club said she was ready for a new challenge and applied to become the manager of our hotel there; she's now doing brilliantly in her new role.

But to return to what I was saying earlier, I can't stress enough the importance of delegation. It has freed me up to think strategically and move the company forward, and in that respect has been central to my success. Our company structure is robust because everyone knows their role and their importance to the company as a whole. Crucially, they know they are trusted to do their jobs well.

However, now that the company is relatively stable, I know I'm not the best person to be in charge as it doesn't suit my personality. Nigel does a much better job running the business than I would, although I hope he'd say I'm still useful to bounce ideas off. Then again, he might not. If I really did go and sit on a beach for a year, I know I wouldn't have to worry about the business because Nigel and the rest of my team are all so fantastic at what they do.

THIRTY

Heartbroken

Normally I can pop in and out of the office without people noticing, but there was one day in October 2012 when I unintentionally created a bit of a scene. It was at a time when the negotiations over the divorce were getting very tense and it was starting to take a toll on my health.

I was sitting at my desk going through some correspondence. I was getting quite used to feeling angry by this point, but on this particular morning I didn't just feel the usual mix of rage and sadness, I felt pain. It was right across my chest and down into my fused vertebrae and it was really, really bad. I buzzed Kim, who came into my office straight away.

'I'm having chest pains.' It was actually quite hard to talk through the pain.

'Should I call an ambulance?'

That seemed a bit extreme, but I knew I needed help.

'I'll call your doctor.'

Kim was great. She got straight on the phone to my GP

and described what I was experiencing. My doctor said that with chest pains like that you should always call 999, which is what Kim did. Meanwhile the pain became all-encompassing and I had to stay completely still to be able to breathe. Knowing that help was on its way alleviated my panic a little, but the pain was immense.

I was worried because about eight years previously I had been told at my annual check-up that I have a minor heart abnormality: the left side of my heart is bigger than the right. It doesn't cause me any trouble, it just means my heart has a slightly unusual rhythm. But what was really frightening me as I sat there struggling to draw breath was something else the doctor had said. After examining my test results, he turned to me and said:

'When did you have your heart attack?'

'I never have,' I told him.

He told me my scan results showed that I had. 'You must have had a silent heart attack.'

'What's that?'

He explained that it's possible to have a heart attack and not know about it. You might experience chest pains, but they pass before you think to call a doctor or an ambulance. I then remembered a time driving home from the Lakes about ten years previously when I'd had the most terrible, terrible pains. I'll never know if that was my silent attack but it seems quite likely. Knowing that I had had a heart attack in the past added considerably to my anxiety as Kim and I waited for an ambulance.

Luckily it turned out that there was one just round the corner at a petrol station and within five minutes two paramedics were in my office. They listened to my heartbeat and put a pill under my tongue to relieve the pain. There's something about having the paramedics there that helps you to relax. The pain started to subside and I began to feel quite sure I wasn't having a heart attack. I wondered if instead it was something related to my horse-riding accident.

'I think I'm going to be all right,' I said.

'You're still going to hospital,' they said.

'But I'm feeling better.'

'There are tests you need to have in hospital that will let us know exactly what's going on.'

Of course, while all this was happening inside my office, gossip had started within the building that an ambulance had been called, and that it had been called for me. I wasn't aware of that at the time – and I had completely forgotten that my daughter Jennifer was working in the building.

The paramedics strapped me into a wheelchair (I wasn't allowed to walk) and took me out of my office, down in the lift and out into the ambulance. It was only then that I realised people had started to rubberneck to see what was going on. I later found out that Jennifer had seen the ambulance drive away and had asked who it had been called for. Ed, our lawyer, had to tell her it was for her dad.

I was taken to the local A&E unit where they monitored my heart rate and told me that everything looked fine.

'Yeah, I feel fine now. I think I've wasted everyone's time. I should probably get back to work.'

'You're not going anywhere for at least 12 hours.' It was explained to me that a heart attack leaves a trace of something in your blood that can be detected after 12 hours with a simple test. 'But as that will be about 1am, I think we can safely say you'll be spending the night in here.'

Jennifer arrived, and I think I was as relieved to see her as she was to see me. She arranged for some things to be brought for me from home and I got ready to spend a night in hospital. I don't have medical insurance, as I prefer to pay if and when I need treatment, but the hospital found me a private room without my asking for it. I think they realised it wasn't a good time for people to be asking if they could have their picture taken with me. I was very grateful for their thoughtfulness.

The test was done in the middle of the night and it confirmed that I hadn't had a heart attack, but I was also told that a cardiologist had a vacancy in his clinic the following day and they wanted to keep me in to see him.

So the next day I was introduced to the heart specialist, who turned out to be the same doctor who had told me about my silent attack.

'Your heart's fine,' he said after putting me through a series of tests. 'What you experienced yesterday was a stress attack, a panic attack. There's nothing wrong with you physically, but you need to work out what's causing you so much stress.'

I explained that the source of my stress was simple: divorce.

Knowing that – stress aside – I was in good health helped me to stay positive and that in turn brought my stress levels down. However, I did have one minor irritation to deal with – the press. I had tweeted my friend Peter Jinks while I was in my hospital bed, and some journalists had picked up on it. When Jennifer came in to see me she said there were quite a few gentlemen of the press outside. Normally I'm quite happy to speak to journalists but it really wasn't the time or the place. They found a back door I could leave by.

In the following days, I received lots of cards and emails from well-wishers but one stands out – it was from Gordon Brown. He had seen the press reports and wanted to let me know that I was in his thoughts. It was a lovely gesture. Although I didn't rate him very highly as Prime Minister, I've always liked him personally – that's one of the reasons I campaigned with him in the 2010 election. Obviously he isn't quite as busy since he left office, but I was still touched that he had cared enough to write to me.

A few weeks later, when I had recovered, it occurred to me that if I really had been having a heart attack, I would have had a much greater chance of survival if everyone in the company knew first aid. We are now one of the few companies where every member of staff gets trained by St John Ambulance. I might not have needed that expertise, but one day someone else might.

I suppose it's inevitable that the older I get, the more health problems I'm going to have. Stress attacks aside, I take very good care of myself and see a personal trainer several times a week, but there's no doubt that it's becoming harder to keep fit. There are definitely mornings when it doesn't seem as easy to get out of bed any more – but they just remind me of the importance of my training sessions.

In 2013, my age seemed to be catching up with me when I realised that I hadn't slept through a night for months. I kept getting up to go to the loo, something that is apparently very common as men get older. My doctor sent me for an extremely painful probe where it was discovered that I had an enlarged prostate. This wasn't a big surprise, given how many times I was getting up in the night, but it was a little unnerving when the doctor told me they needed to take a biopsy to make sure it wasn't cancerous.

It was obviously a big relief when the results came back negative, but by that time the drugs I had been prescribed to reduce the size of my prostate had started to work. That meant I had already started to sleep through the night again, and I almost immediately found I had more energy. It just goes to show what a difference it makes if you take care of yourself.

I still have the annual check-ups that diagnosed my irregular heartbeat all those years ago, which means any issues are picked up before they become problematic. I would advise anyone who can afford it to get one. The past couple of years have shown me that some risks just aren't worth taking.

THIRTY-ONE

All Eyes on 2016

In addition to the divorce, there was another source of stress I was dealing with in 2012 – the IBRC valuers. They were still desperate to show that we were in breach of our covenants and so they wanted to exercise their right to an annual valuation of the business. We received a letter in May or June that year notifying us of their intention to start the process again in August. I was just getting so fed up with it all.

Knowing that I had absolutely no spare cash, we realised we wouldn't have any flexibility if they found us in breach by a couple of million as they had done the year before. If they did – and if they could prove that we really were in breach – then they would be entitled to call in the loan, which could in theory be fatal for Bannatyne Fitness.

The one thing it was in our power to do was to reduce the debt further, so we took the decision sell the London flat, which was a company property. We needed to stall the valuers until that cash was in the bank, but – despite headlines you might have read about the London property market soaring in the face of a national decline – selling the flat wouldn't be easy. Although there were plenty of people who wanted to buy it, lenders were getting increasingly strict about their lending criteria. We knew it would take several months, and so yet again we went through the farce of explaining that they couldn't possibly value property X on date Y because we simply didn't have anyone to show them round.

Selling the London flat wasn't a big wrench for me. It had been Joanne's idea to buy in Covent Garden and although I enjoyed having London on my doorstep it was not the most convenient area to get in and out of. And now that *Dragons' Den* has moved to Salford, I'm not often in London anyway, so using hotels makes much more sense – it simply means remembering to pack a toothbrush. The flat had become far more valuable to me as cash and I just wanted it sold.

Once we completed the sale and the money was in the bank, we eased up on the stalling tactics and the bank was able to complete its valuation. Even though we were continuing to pay back £2.5 million every three months, they still found us in breach. I was as stunned as I was angry. They really didn't care about the jobs they were putting in jeopardy or the damage they were doing to the business. Our only option was to fight.

We went through their valuation looking for every possible error and after a week or so – we were in no hurry, remember – we wrote to them explaining a number of ways in which we felt they had failed to complete their valuation properly. We identified several plots of land we owned that they had omitted.

They wrote back and said OK, they would value those new plots but the valuer needed £25,000 to carry out the valuation. After taking several deep breaths we calmly replied, pointing out that our loan agreement only says we have to pay for the annual valuation. Any additional valuations, we argued, therefore had to be carried out at their own expense.

At every stage, letters went back and forth, and every time that happened we knew we were buying ourselves more time. By the time they visited and valued the other sites, we had paid off another £2.5 million and they had to accept we weren't in breach.

It's impossible not to look back on the Anglo Irish deal we did in 2006 and wonder if we would be better off had we never bought the LivingWell clubs. Bannatyne Fitness would be a much smaller company making smaller profits, but at least we would have had several lenders and several different repayment dates and there wouldn't be one bank with such power over our future. I have to say that when we did the deal in 2006, I don't think anyone in the company foresaw that we would be put in such a difficult situation.

On New Year's Eve 2012 I held a big party at my house to celebrate the fact that what I felt had been the worst year of my life was behind me. The details of my divorce had just been agreed: with that and the reprieve from the valuers, I was very ready to start looking forward.

When we returned to the office in January 2013, I decided it was time to sit down with my team to start plotting a course through the years ahead. We had to accept that IBRC were going to try to call in the loan at every opportunity and that every year we would have to be ready for their valuers. I also realised that we have another problem: if the lending climate doesn't improve, there is a real possibility that when our loan period ends in August 2016 we might not be able to borrow the £90 million we will still owe IBRC – even though our assets have recently been valued at £217 million.

The thought that IBRC could force the sale of the company in 2016 is really quite terrifying. They would be under no obligation to sell it to the highest bidder. It's not uncommon for banks and their liquidators to recover precisely the amount they need and no more (you may think this is evidence of dodgy practices but I couldn't possibly comment) and if someone offered them £90 million they would happily take it. If that happened, I could lose every asset I have and still be in debt. I would be left with nothing. Not a single penny. Zero. Zilch.

I can live without money, but I feel an enormous responsibility to my children not to let that happen. I do not want to let them down. But if there's one good thing to come out of my divorce it's that it has reignited my fighting spirit. At an age when other people might be thinking about retiring, I am supremely motivated to make a massive success out of the next few years. I have a tremendous desire to take the company forward and grow it again.

Previously, I had thought that a time would come when I would want to sell the company, and that I would leave the majority of my wealth to the Bannatyne Trust. But after what has happened over the last few years, I am absolutely determined to leave a legacy for my children.

It was with this in mind that I sat down in January with Nigel, Chris (my finance director) and Ed (our in-house lawyer). Between us, I wanted us to find a way to get into a position where we could refinance our debt, and release a bit of cash for me, as I'd been surviving on credit cards. I needed to liquidate some of my assets.

I already had a good idea of what our options would be, but it was an incredibly creative meeting where everyone had valuable contributions to make. I'm sure it must have made a difference that we had recently moved into our new HQ. It's not a flash building – there's no bucking bronco in the canteen or fountain in reception – but compared to our old offices our new HQ feels like a place where things happen. I've never been an advocate of spending money on premises unnecessarily – certainly at the start-up stage – but since we've moved into our new building, you can almost feel the positivity and the self-belief. Without anyone having said anything, I've noticed that our staff have started to dress more smartly: there's a new pride and determination in the workforce, and it's infectious. The four of us sat round the table and pitched in one suggestion after another.

Over the next few weeks, as I kept looking back to my notes from that meeting, I realised that we had actually developed a seven-point plan. The more I looked at it, the more I knew that step by step, point by point, we were going to get to that August 2016 deadline in fantastic shape.

THIRTY-TWO

The Seven-Point Plan

Our priority was to shore up Bannatyne Fitness, and our key objective was to reduce our borrowing in that company as much as possible. It was a difficult conversation but we all realised what we were saying: if we had to sell the hotels to save the health clubs, then that was what we would do. We all knew that at the end of the process, the Bannatyne Group might look very different, but we could also see that it would be a much stronger company.

Point One on our master plan was to sell off any non-revenue-producing assets. I suppose it's the business equivalent of selling the things in your attic that you haven't used for years and you're never likely to use. What we were looking for wasn't necessarily the assets that could release the most cash – although that would be nice – but the assets that, once disposed of, would cause the least disruption to the business. Our old offices in Darlington, for instance, have been lying empty since we moved into our new HQ:

we have no need for them any more so it makes sense to put them on the market. Most of the assets were plots of land we had acquired when we'd built our clubs that had been surplus to requirements. At one point we'd had plans to build on them, but the harsh lending climate meant that was no longer an option. We hadn't needed to sell them before, but now that we did, we called up our agents and told them we were open to offers.

At the back of our Mansfield club, for instance, there are some old tennis courts that we got planning permission to build housing on before the crash. It became unviable to do in the years that followed. I instructed Ed, our in-house lawyer, to put the land up for sale and we got interest from a developer who wanted to make changes to our plans. If he can get his own plans approved then he'll buy the land. It'll bring in the best part of £1 million.

We also got an approach from someone wanting to buy just a corner of a plot we own in Burton upon Trent. They offered us £87,000 for it. It's not the kind of money that will get us out of trouble with the banks, but in our current mindset we are pursuing every single opportunity to get cash onto our books. We said yes.

Next to our Newcraighall club in Edinburgh is a Premier Inn and they said they would buy some parking spaces from us so they could expand. Again, it wasn't a lot of money in relation to the amounts we are dealing with – a little under £200,000 – but we agreed to the deal.

When we bought the LivingWell clubs, we also acquired their offices in Milton Keynes. We'd never had any need for them, and they had been empty ever since we bought them.

They were put up for sale or rent and we got an offer from a lap-dancing club operator.

We always knew the parcel of land that was potentially our most valuable was at our Grove Park club in south-east London. It's a 13-acre site that is suitable for housing. When the headlines were full of stories about planning legislation being relaxed, we were approached by an agent who thought he could get planning permission on some of it. As soon as he does – it's still going through at the time of writing – those 13 acres could be worth as much as £10 million.

Altogether, we identified a substantial number of valuable non-revenue-producing assets – a pretty successful attic sale. If all the sales are secured, it should mean we will never risk being in breach of our covenants again, and it will make it much easier to refinance the entire loan, if and when that time comes.

Point Two on our master plan is to sell any Bannatyne Fitness assets that are revenue-generative to one of our other companies. The IBRC loan is with Bannatyne Fitness 1, so if Bannatyne Fitness 2 buys some of the clubs, that takes the debt out of Bannatyne Fitness 1 and puts a big cushion between the company and the bank's covenants. This is something we are actively pursuing at the time of writing.

Point Three is to sell assets in either Bannatyne Hotels or Bannatyne Properties that we can get ten times profits for. We will then use that money to do more of what we're already doing in Point Two.

This isn't a fire sale. We aren't going to sell anything for less than the best price. When we talked through our options, we all agreed that it made sense to sell hotels rather than health clubs for the very simple reason that hotels are valued at ten times profit, whereas the clubs are more like eight times profit.

So we reluctantly put Charlton House on the market with a price tag of £3.5 million. I think the highest bid we received was £3 million, but we said we weren't selling at that price and took it off the market. I have even considered putting the Darlington hotel on the market. Given that it is the hotel I have owned the longest and the one in my home town, this is not something I'm doing without a lot of thought. But I can't be emotional about it. Ultimately business is about numbers, and if we get the right price we'll sell. I suppose the good thing about having been in business for so long is that I know there will be other ventures and other purchases. I don't get sentimental about it anymore – it's just business.

Every company is helped by having clear objectives and right now our objective is stark: raise cash, and then use that cash to secure lending so one of our other companies can buy assets from Bannatyne Fitness 1. Everything is now focused on getting our borrowing down to a level where I can get another bank to lend me the money to pay off IBRC. It's as simple as that.

Point Four is something I didn't think I'd ever consider, but at the end of our meeting I realised it was now something I had to embrace: sale and leaseback. Throughout my career, I have always enjoyed running businesses where I own the assets. Other people might want to lease an ice-cream van but my instinct was to buy one. I owned the freeholds of the care homes we built and the hotels we bought. I also owned the freeholds of the health clubs we built – the only reason

Bannatyne Fitness owned any leasehold clubs was because they had been part of acquisitions.

The reason I like owning freeholds is twofold: firstly, your business is worth more because of the multiple of profits you can use to determine a sale price; secondly, at some point you pay off the debt – just like a mortgage on your home – and you own it outright. When that happens, your profits surge and you have an extremely valuable business. However, it's not a model many people use because most people think in a much more short-term way than I do.

A leaseback agreement would involve selling the freehold to another company, and then leasing it back from them at an agreed amount each year. In the short term it's great because you get the money from selling the freehold, but in the long term you are vulnerable to rent rises that could put you out of business. It's also a form of secret debt: it doesn't show on your books, but you will be paying rent forever rather than paying off the loans. Rent is just another form of long-term debt and isn't that much different from off-balance-sheet accounting, where your debts are hidden from this year's figures but they will still – and will always – need to be paid.

People who have read *Anyone Can Do It* will know what a change of attitude it is for me to consider leasebacks, but it makes such sense for us now that I am becoming really passionate about it. Once we've sold the freeholds, we'll use the money to reduce the size of our borrowing which makes us less vulnerable to interest-rate rises in the future. Given the lending climate, that's now a very sensible position to take. But there is another financial advantage to doing leasebacks. Let's say you run a company that makes £15 million in profit a year but you have loan repayments of £10 million a year. You'll pay 23% corporation tax on the £15 million and so you're left with just over £1.5 million. Now let's say you sell your freeholds and instead of repaying a loan you pay rent instead. You still make £15 million a year but you pay £10 million in rent; now you'll only pay corporation tax on the remaining £5 million, leaving you with £3.85 million after tax. Although your pre-tax profits drop from £15 million to £5 million, your cash flow more than doubles.

At Bannatyne Fitness, I have never needed the cash available before, but I do now and so doing leasebacks finally makes sense. Finding buyers in this climate should be fairly straightforward as there are lots of investors who are looking for guaranteed income, whether it's a pension fund or a rich oligarch who wants more of a return – and more security – than a bank can offer. The crucial thing for us is choosing the right clubs to sell.

After the meeting in January, our finance team did a series of calculations to identify which of our clubs could be sold for the most money in relation to the valuation the bank had placed on them. We then contracted Christie's to arrange the sale and leaseback of twenty-four properties. They were a mix of freehold and leasehold that Christie's valued at £92 million. When the sale goes through, we'll have a contract with the new owners to pay a fixed rent of just under £7 million per annum for a fixed number of years, with rent rises and reassessments agreed in advance over a 25-year period. They get a regular income and a valuable asset, and we get to reduce our borrowing and massively increase our cash flow. Right now, that looks like a very good deal indeed and if it all goes through it will go a long way to wiping out our debt. You can understand why I'm so keen to press ahead with it.

Point Five is to sell some of our clubs to other operators. Nigel has put out feelers, but at the time of writing there haven't been any takers.

Point Six is to find someone to refinance the Anglo Irish/IBRC debt. Given the lending situation, that may mean doing deals with private individuals or companies, so we could see ourselves in partnership with a Qatari equity fund or a Russian oligarch.

Point Seven, and I can't quite believe I'm writing this, is to sell the company. Obviously this is something I do not want to do, but if there's still a chance that IBRC could force a sale between now and 2016 that could leave me with nothing, then it's an option I can no longer rule out.

THIRTY-THREE

The Best-Laid Plans

Some of the decisions we made in that meeting were incredibly painful, but they nonetheless made me feel very positive about the future. We had a problem, but we had also identified several solutions, and I felt confident that I had a brilliant team who were all focused on the right things. Everything was going to be OK. The company was going to be fine. I was going to be fine. New year, new start, new successes.

On the other side of the Irish Sea, however, events were taking place that could potentially mean tearing up our brilliant seven-point plan. At the beginning of February 2013, the Irish government announced it had negotiated with the European Central Bank to wind up the Irish Bank Resolution Corporation and hand over its assets to a newly recreated 'bad bank' called the National Asset Management Agency. NAMA was effectively charged with calling in bad debts for the good of the nation. Although this would create problems for us, I could see it also had the potential to be a welcome piece of news.

I was told that the liquidator – KPMG – had been brought in to sell all the debt because it was costing money for the bank to continue to operate. There was no point having a head office and all the other support services if it was no longer lending money – all that was doing was wasting money.

The liquidator had been instructed by the Irish government to sell all the bank's assets by the end of August before closing it down (the deadline has since been put back to the end of 2013). One of those assets is the £120 million still owed to them by Bannatyne Fitness. In the current climate, they would have to be realistic about what they could actually get for their outstanding loans. Perhaps they would calculate that it was better to have £100 million in their hand, rather than £120 million on their books. The exact discount they would accept would be a difficult calculation, but we definitely saw that there would be a chance to reduce our borrowing. Under EU law, the bank manager told me, the liquidators would have to offer us a chance to buy our debts before offering them to the highest bidder.

This was the kind of opportunity that could potentially transform the business. Not only was there a realistic chance of buying £120 million worth of debt for less than face value, but we could free ourselves from the threat of annual valuations. There were just two very big questions we had to answer: how much would they accept, and who on earth would lend us the money to buy the debt?

I tried to put myself in the liquidators' position to estimate the value they would put on a sale of the loan. I had a few things in my favour. Firstly, we were paying a very low interest rate. The fact that I had a contract for another three and a half years meant that they couldn't call in the full amount any time soon. And given the state of international finance, they wouldn't have much confidence that they would get a better price if they waited until 2016. If I was working for the liquidators, I think I would be inclined to negotiate a deal now at a lower price than let the loan run its course.

There is always a fine balance to be struck when negotiating something like this. If you make too low an offer, you risk them opening it out to highest bidders. If you bid too high, you incur unnecessary costs. My guess was that an offer in the region of 75% stood a good chance of being accepted. If we were successful in buying the £120 million loan for £90 million, it would mean we had just wiped £30 million off our debts. But there was still that second question to be answered: who was going to lend us £90 million in this climate? We needed a specialist financier to tell us.

We spoke to a number of brokers, some of whom thought 75% was too high. In our initial discussions, I considered that presented an opportunity to incentivise them to negotiate the best possible deal. We were prepared to pay 75%: we could share anything they could negotiate below that level, potentially getting them a massive bonus.

There were two potential sources of finding £90 million: the first was another bank, and the second was a private company or individual. Buying the debt at a discount would mean our loan-to-value – the ratio of debt to assets in the business – would drop to around 40%. That would give a lender a great deal of security – if they had £90 million to lend. As it's still the case that banks are reluctant to make loans as they continue the process of recapitalisation, finding money privately was an option worth investigation.

It's well known that the UK, and London in particular, has become home to increasing numbers of billionaires – Russian oligarchs, Qatari princes and the like – many of whom are interested in finding alternative places to put their money. At the time we were having these initial discussions with our brokers, the financial crisis had moved to Cyprus, where the big headline was that wealthy Russian depositors had lost billions when the state seized money from their bank accounts to secure a bailout from the EU. All of a sudden, the prospect of lending money to a private company like ours was looking like a safer bet.

We still had to make it worth someone's while, however, and I proposed that if someone would buy our debts for £90 million, we would make payments on £100 million. We would effectively give them an extra £10 million over the life of the loan, on top of any interest of course. It seemed to me to be a very good deal for both parties: they make £10 million overnight, and we save £20 million at the same time.

I've made it sound very simple, but these are not the kinds of deals that happen with a handshake over a pint in the pub. Getting access to individuals and companies that might want to participate in deals like these isn't easy. You need to know the right people who move in the right circles and who can open the right doors. They are the sorts of deals that have to be brokered in the right way.

In the meantime, my team is focused on making whatever

the final deal is as attractive as possible. If we raise £92 million from asset disposal, sale and leasebacks, then our LTV ratio will be so low that we could probably borrow whatever we needed from a high street lender.

By May 2013, we had agreed the sale of several of our assets but then ran into an unexpected problem: the liquidators for the bank wouldn't sign off the sales. Just as a mortgage company has to give permission when you sell a house, we needed our lender's authority to complete the sales.

I emailed the liquidator three times but never heard back from him. It got to the stage where potential buyers for other assets were asking for evidence we'd get the lender's permission before we all went to the expense of drawing up contracts. This was absolutely crazy – not to mention completely unacceptable – because we were offering to repay the loan at a pound for a pound. There was no discount to negotiate at this stage, we simply wanted to repay a portion of our debt but they wouldn't let us!

In the end I went on Twitter and said that any Irish followers I had should know that the liquidators had turned down our money, and that the Irish people should be worried. I got several replies along the lines of 'the Irish government has been screwing us over for so long it's not a surprise', and within a few hours I had given interviews to Irish newspapers and the articles started to appear online.

Now, it may be a complete and utter coincidence, but before those articles ended up in the following day's news-papers, I finally got a reply from the liquidator. Perhaps the minister of finance had called him. Perhaps he feared the bad publicity, or maybe he was due to get back to me that day anyway. I'll never know, but I did finally get permission to sell those assets, and our seven-point plan started to shape up nicely.

THIRTY-FOUR

Learning to Smile

Shortly after reaching an agreement with the liquidators, I took a trip to Guadalajara in Mexico where I have a long-standing commitment to help a charity called Operation Smile UK. About 18 months beforehand, I had been at a charity auction and paid £11,000 to win a week observing the charity's work at first hand. The divorce and financial situation had meant I'd had to delay the trip several times, so I was thrilled to finally be flying out there and getting involved.

Operation Smile repairs cleft palates and cleft lips for children and adults in about 60 countries around the world. All their surgeons, anaesthetists and nursing staff are volunteers. In the UK, these operations are often done soon after birth, but in countries where there is no national health service, thousands of children miss out on potentially life-saving surgery, and thousands more adults are shunned by people throughout their lives or suffer unnecessary side effects.

On one of my first trips to a Romanian orphanage in the 1990s, I had met a lovely little girl who was deaf and blind because she'd had food trapped in her cleft palate that had gone unnoticed. The resulting infection had eventually caused her disabilities. It was so unnecessary, and it was one of the reasons I was so motivated to find out more about how Operation Smile makes a difference.

It was a 22-hour trip to reach Guadalajara, where Operation Smile had set up a week-long clinic at which they hoped to perform surgery on 118 patients. Many children and their parents travelled for hours to reach the clinic, often on overcrowded and unreliable buses. For most of them, this was their only hope of getting a life-changing operation for the child.

Alex Talbot from Operation Smile UK travelled with me and she suggested that I follow the journeys of a handful of children from their arrival at the hospital through to having their operations. The clinic had set up a number of 'stations' to assess the suitability of the child for surgery. The first few stations dealt with paperwork, the next few measured height, weight and blood pressure, then they took blood tests, and if the child made it that far they finally got to see one of Operation Smile's surgeons who would decide if they could receive treatment.

As I said, the specialists and staff were all volunteers and they came from all over the world. They brought their own instruments with them, even their own sutures, which is why Operation Smile is able to carry out cleft-lip repairs for as little as £150 (cleft-palate operations are more complicated – some clefts go all the way up to the skull – and cost considerably more). Some volunteers – like me – weren't medically trained, but we all helped to keep the children entertained and relaxed in what could otherwise have been a frightening situation for them and their parents.

One of the first children I got to know was Dulce Maria, who was only seven months old. Her mother, Lisbeth, was just 17. Dulce had what is called a bilateral cleft lip, which means a separation on both the left and right sides of the lip. Dulce and Lisbeth had travelled for 12 hours by bus to reach the clinic. I sat with them as they went through the first few stations and was with them when they met Mr Sarmiento, the surgeon. The good news was that he could see no reason why Dulce shouldn't have the operation. The only potential problem was identified by the anaesthetist, who was worried that Lisbeth's asthma could have been passed on to Dulce, but her blood tests suggested this probably wasn't the case. As I sat looking at Lisbeth with her daughter on her knee, I calculated that it had been 20 hours since they'd got on the bus, and in the whole time they had been at the clinic I hadn't seen them eat or drink anything. Dulce was such a well-behaved little girl. It was an incredibly emotional few hours, and when I got back to my hotel in the evening I just wanted to cry. I can only imagine what Lisbeth must have been feeling. After all, every child attending the clinic would benefit from surgery – but there were 410 of them, and only enough time to perform 118 operations.

The surgeons reluctantly had to turn down children for a variety of reasons. Some children were undernourished and simply not strong enough to undergo treatment, and where this was the case, the parents would be given nutritional information in the hope that their child could be operated on a few months down the line. Sometimes, the surgery was just too complicated to be carried out at the clinic as too much aftercare would be needed. It's like a very serious and heartbreaking version of the *X Factor*, but there's no public vote, and no matter how much some stories tugged at the surgeons' heartstrings, they still had to reject very worthy contenders.

Lisbeth told me she had friends she could stay with in Guadalajara until the surgeons announced who would be selected in a few days' time.

I also spent time with Jocelyn, who was six months old, blind and orphaned. She held my finger tightly as I talked to her guardian while the medics assessed her at the various stations. Sadly, the medical team deemed she was too unwell for surgery.

My heart went out to this little girl, so I went to visit the orphanage where she is looked after. Compared to the orphanages I had seen in Romania nearly 20 years before, this place was clean and bright and I left there feeling confident that Jocelyn would get the medicine she needed – and after that, I hoped she'd get her surgery too.

'Decision day' was one of the most emotional days of my life – I cannot imagine what it must have been like for the children and parents. There were 410 families waiting for their child's name to be called out, and while we all shared in the elation of those who had made the list, we also shared the pain of those who didn't. I spent decision day with a two-year-old boy called Dilan and his parents. Dilan's lip and top gum were very badly distorted and they had been waiting to hear his fate for four hours. Earlier in the week, the doctors had prescribed medication for Dilan, and his parents were waiting to find out if this had made enough of a difference for him to make the list. When his name was read out, his mum jumped for joy. His dad and I both started crying.

I went with Dilan into the operating theatre where I saw the incredible skill of the surgeons. Operation Smile was started by an American surgeon called Bill Magee 30 years ago, and Bill was doing some of the surgery in Guadalajara, alongside his son Billy who has followed in his father's footsteps. They were both incredible guys, and the work they do makes such a difference. It was an honour to see them work, and to carry Dilan out of the theatre and hand him back to his mum.

But it was a day of mixed emotions. Dulce had been selected for surgery but she and Lisbeth didn't turn up. The charity called Lisbeth but didn't get an answer. Maybe she hadn't been able to stay in Guadalajara after all, or maybe she couldn't afford another bus fare, or maybe she had got frightened – I'll never know. But now that Dulce is on Operation Smile's books, she should be invited for follow-up appointments and there will hopefully be another chance for her to have her surgery.

One of the great things about Operation Smile is that during their week-long clinic, they taught several local surgeons how to carry out repairs to cleft lips and palates. Sharing knowledge and skills is an important part of the charity's work, and the real legacy of our week in Mexico isn't just the new smiles on 118 children's faces, it's the fact that there is now a weekly cleft lip and palate clinic in the city, where they aim to carry out four surgeries a week. I really hope that Dulce will be at one of them.

I returned to the UK completely energised and fired up. A few days later I received the wonderful news that Jocelyn had returned to the clinic and was now well enough to have her surgery. I realised I wanted to do more to support Operation Smile. And the best way to do that was to make more profits so the Bannatyne Foundation could make ongoing donations. Yet another reason that I am determined to ensure the business thrives.

THIRTY-FIVE

Where it All Went Wrong – and How to Put it Right

Spending so much time lately with financiers and brokers has made it a little easier to understand why the economy got into such a mess in the first place. Products got too complicated and people got too cocky. It doesn't seem very long ago that the image of a banker was a risk-averse pen-pusher only interested in making moderate, safe returns. Anyone under the age of 30 now thinks of bankers as adrenaline-addicted risk-takers who are only out for themselves.

I am often asked for my view of why things went wrong, and I used to answer that I was just a simple man, trying to run a straightforward business – not an expert on complicated finance. These days though, being in business requires an understanding of finance that was not needed when I started out. It's something I've been struggling to get my head round for a while and I think I've now come up with a few ideas that could help get us out of this mess and ensure it doesn't happen again.

A few years ago, I wrote an article for the *Daily Telegraph* saying that the biggest cause of trouble was the fact that banks all lent money to each other. I said in that piece that I thought there should be a new law that made the banks all operate independently, like supermarkets. If Sainsbury's lent money to Tesco, and Tesco lent money to the Co-op and then one of them went bust, then they'd all go bust. I knew I was onto something when Deborah Meaden said she agreed with me. If you get Deborah's support you know you're making sense and if they ever make me Chancellor, I'm going to appoint Deborah as Chief Secretary to the Treasury!

It's a ridiculous situation to have the banks tumbling down because they are so intricately connected, and I don't see that all the bailouts and all the new regulations have really dealt with the issue. If they were separate and self contained, then there would still be healthy banks left to buy the ones that go bust. If Sainsbury's went bust, Morrisons would buy some of their shops. Independence is much healthier than interdependence.

When Bannatyne Fitness borrowed £180 million from Anglo Irish, I don't think we were naive to think they were lending us money that was actually theirs to lend. We didn't know that they didn't have it and they were borrowing from other institutions. It's as if the money didn't exist or we were all playing some financial version of pass the parcel, only when the last layer of wrapping paper was removed there was just an IOU. They were offering loans with other people's money and it hasn't just caused problems for us, but also for thousands of other companies that borrowed from them.

Another rule I'd like to bring in is that banks should have to adhere to the same LTV levels they impose on the companies they lend to. Anglo Irish wanted us to ensure that our lending represented no more than 58% of the value of the business. Imagine if they had to make sure their LTV ratio was that high. There wouldn't have been a financial crisis.

I have to admit, though, I don't quite understand who they owe the money to. Is it the Russians? China? The Arabs? In business, if someone owes you money and fails to pay, you take them to court. If they won't pay, you seize their assets. But I don't see any court cases; I'm not reading stories about assets being repatriated. What country is saying they want their money back? After five or six years of the financial crisis I still haven't met anyone who truly fully understands it.

In 2009, I wrote a book called *How To Be Smart With Your Money*. I tried to explain that looking after money isn't as complex or intimidating as many people think and that by adopting a few basic rules it's possible to make money work harder for you. Not long after it was published, I was invited to join Gordon Brown at Chequers. I went with my son Tom, who's almost the same age as Gordon's sons. As this was before the divorce and the revaluations, we went by helicopter. After we landed on the lawn at Chequers, Gordon came to greet us and Tom gave him a gift – a copy of *How To Be Smart With Your Money*! I'm guessing that he didn't read it, given the state we're in.

That said, I think he was right to take a stake in the

bailed-out banks – but I think he and Alistair Darling made a mistake by not changing the way they paid the directors of those banks. Instead of paying them an annual bonus, I think they should have told the new chief executives that their job was to sell the British taxpayers' stake for a profit and that they could keep 10% of whatever the country made. They could get paid £100 million so long as that meant the taxpayer had made £900 million. There's no point in paying a bonus related to the share price as that is too volatile and too easy to manipulate: bonuses for the senior directors at the nationalised banks should only be linked to the taxpayers' return on investment.

I remember talking to Gordon Brown about what amounted to a cash-flow problem at the Treasury. Basically, people and businesses weren't paying the taxes they owed quickly enough. 'Give them an incentive then,' I said. 'If I sold a business today, I wouldn't have to hand over the capital gains tax until after I've filed my next tax return. Why don't you introduce a system where you pay less if you pay it sooner?'

Despite my criticisms of Gordon Brown, I have to say that he is responsible for the single most important change in economic policy in my lifetime. When Labour came to power in 1997, one of the first things he did was to give independence to the Bank of England to set interest rates. Until then, interest rates always came down before an election and went straight back up after the polls closed. That single change has meant we've had stable interest rates for the past 15 years, and that has been great for businesses. Nor does Gordon Brown get nearly enough credit for not taking us into the euro, which most commentators seem to think Tony Blair was very keen on.

What matters now is that we all – businesses and governments – learn from what has gone wrong. As well as legislating to keep the banks' finances separate, I think there's more to be done to keep the wealth of banks and bankers more closely interlinked. The proposals to limit the size of bonuses to a multiple of annual salary don't really deal with the fundamental problem that individual bankers will favour the chance to make money for themselves in the short term over the bank's profits in the long term. Just like when employees steal money from the till, the personal gain for taking the risk is too great in relation to the damage done to the company. We need legislation to ensure that what is in the banks' interest is also in the bankers' interest.

As my team implements our seven-point plan, it's interesting how often my mind wanders back to the conversation I had with Allied Irish Bank in 2006 about Anglo Irish 'punching above their weight'. So I suppose the other lesson we all need to learn is that if something seems too good to be true, there's a bloody good reason for it. I don't think I ever really believed Gordon Brown when he said his policies would put an end to 'boom and bust', but I certainly didn't see the bust coming. (Although, to be fair to him, the boom is over – he was half right!) Looking back, it's clear there were a few signs that the economy wasn't as healthy as we thought, and the next time credit becomes easily available, action must be taken to avoid the same thing happening again. The question for me is, where will I be when it happens?

THIRTY-SIX

What's Next?

It's very hard for me to say how I would have responded to the financial crisis if I had been 30 when it hit. Would I have made different decisions? Quite possibly. But I'm 64 and I've got to think about my children and grandchildren. When our loan period expires in 2016, I'll be 67. That's not a time of life when you want to be thinking about starting over.

Of course, on the home front, that's exactly what I've been forced to do. I didn't want to get divorced – I loved being married and I miss it now – and there's a part of me that can feel quite lost these days. I didn't expect my life to be like this at this age. I no longer have the villa, I don't have the flat in London and I no longer go home to my wife and kids. I spend more nights than I would like in a hotel, living out of a suitcase. I look back on my life before the divorce and I miss it. I really do.

The divorce continues to have an impact on my life. I don't think you ever really get over something so traumatic, especially when there are constant reminders. In 2013, for instance, I discovered that one of my Twitter trolls was actually a relation of Joanne's by marriage. Using the name @thesaintgeorge – i.e. the dragon slayer – they anonymously wrote a series of bullying tweets, and encouraged others to do the same. When they started to say things that only people very close to me would know, I started investigating who it could be. When one of the other trolls they had associated with revealed @thesaintgeorge's real identity, I have to say it wasn't a total surprise.

I was very pleased that the local police took this behaviour seriously, and when @thesaintgeorge was confronted with the evidence, they confessed. While it was satisfying to have had the matter dealt with, it was a painful reminder of just how badly people can behave.

As the kids get older, and especially with Nigel running the company, I feel new opportunities are starting to open up for me. In spring 2013, I put my Wynyard house up for sale because I'm no longer sure it's where I want to be. Obviously I'll rent somewhere close to Tom and Emily, but now that I have the lodge in the Lakes, it's the perfect place to spend time with my family and the people who matter to me.

Once the sale of the house goes through, I honestly don't know where I will settle. I had thought of moving to the south-west to be near Abigail and my grandchildren, but Abigail has plans to move back to the north-east. I sometimes think about getting a flat in London, or a villa in Portugal, and I've even been house-hunting in South Africa but none of those options feel quite right at the moment (although the prospect of living somewhere warmer is very appealing).

That's probably because what I really want are the things that the divorce has taken away from me. Renting while I wait and see what life throws at me next seems like the sensible option.

There is one obvious benefit to being single, which is that there never seems to be a shortage of women who are interested in a man who is famous for being rich. Funny that. But the women I meet are usually in their twenties and there is never any realistic chance that anything serious will develop. I'd like to meet someone new and settle down, though I'm not sure I'd be in a rush to get married. I would though, absolutely, if the right woman came along. And I really hope she does. In the meantime, I get to spend the time I would have spent with Joanne in the company of my kids and grandchildren.

In May 2013, my mother Jean passed away. Her death wasn't unexpected – she was 87 and had been ill and frail for some time – and in some ways her passing was a kind of relief. I had spent an afternoon with her the week before she died, and she told me that she was ready to go. It was one of those terribly sad situations where there just isn't anything you can do: she had gangrene in her leg and was in a lot of pain as it spread through the rest of her body. She was too frail for surgery, so all we could do was wait. I wasn't with her when she died, but she was surrounded by her other children and most of her grandchildren. She knew she was loved.

In recent years, I had become estranged from two of my brothers, but we were all very civil with one another at the funeral. It was Tom and Emily's first funeral. I think it's really important that children are able to say goodbye to someone they love – and I have to say they both showed incredible maturity. Emily in particular was fantastic – though all my kids were – and in the midst of a sad occasion it was actually lovely to see them with all their cousins, something that doesn't happen often enough.

I found myself thinking about all the things my mum had lived through – the war, the poverty of post-war Glasgow, the hardships of running a home and feeding seven kids when there were no washing machines or labour-saving appliances. It seems like a tough life now, but my mum never complained and I am so grateful to her for her love and dedication.

Her death has also made me think more about my father, who died a quarter of a century ago. After World War II – in which he'd been a prisoner of war in Japan – he'd had a life of physical labour in the Singer factory and died of emphysema just two years after his retirement. I know they both wanted a better life for their kids, and I feel blessed and proud that I have been able to turn my father's name into a brand that is recognised all over the country.

It's also made me think about my own legacy and it has made me even more determined to build the business back up, pay off my debts and leave my children financial security and a charitable foundation that will inspire and motivate them for the rest of their lives. At the age of 64, I don't think I have ever been so determined to succeed, and that determination, that belief, is just getting stronger. I love being at work, and I love knowing that I have the capacity to deal with whatever life throws at me, just as my mum and dad did.

Of course, I also want what every parent wants: to see my children and grandchildren grow up to live happy lives and fulfil their potential. It gives me so much pleasure that three of my daughters now work for the business, but I am just as proud of my fourth daughter, Eve, who has decided that the business is not for her. She wants to work with disadvantaged children, either kids with learning difficulties or those who are terminally ill or who have been abused. It's just fantastic that she knows what she wants to do. If the work experience placements she's had so far are anything to go by, she going to be great at it, too.

It's too soon to say what Emily and Tom will want to do when they are older, but I suspect Tom will want to come and work for what's now become the family business. I already talk to him about the company, and when I told him about the seven-point plan recently he became really quite upset at the thought of having to sell any of the hotels or the health clubs. I suppose he's heard me talk about them all his life, and he genuinely cares about the decisions we take. Whatever choices he eventually makes about his life, I'm sure that he will make me as proud as my older children do, and the same goes for Emily.

This book has focused on my work, and I worry that it might give some people the impression that business comes first. Let me clear up any confusion right now. The past couple of years have taught me how lucky I am to have the amazing love of my friends and family and they always, *always* come first.

In the short term, the business has the 2016 deadline looming over it. I know there is a theoretical risk that if we can't sort out our lending problems, I could be forced to sell the business. But my motivation to make sure that doesn't happen is so strong that I just know it won't. In fact, I am certain that the next few years are going to be great. Now that the seven-point plan is starting to get results, our profits and our valuation are going to soar. I expect to see a headline in next year's Rich List that says 'Bannatyne bounces back!'

I don't say that because I want to carry on making more money, I say it because I want to carry on building businesses and running businesses. Maybe it's because I didn't find the thing I was good at until I was in my thirties, but when you find that thing later in life I think you love it all the more: even in my seventies I'll still be in business. I am an entrepreneur and no matter how tough things get, I will survive.

No one asks an artist why he wants to make another beautiful painting if he's already got enough money to live on. No one asks Tom Jones why he still wants to sing. It's really and truly not about the money, it's about carrying on doing the thing I love. If you snap me in two, you'll find 'entrepreneur' running through me like the letters in a stick of seaside rock.

Index